Study Guide

for

Siegel's

Criminology:
The Core

Second Edition

Laura B. Myers
Prairie View A&M University

Larry J. Myers
Justice Communications Inc.

THOMSON

WADSWORTH

Australia • Canada • Mexico • Singapore • Spain • United Kingdom • United States

Cover Image: Noah Woods

Printed in the United States of America
1 2 3 4 5 6 7 07 06 05 04

Printer: Darby Printing

ISBN: 0-534-62941-5

For more information about our products,
contact us at:
Thomson Learning Academic Resource Center
1-800-423-0563

For permission to use material from this text,
contact us by:
Phone: 1-800-730-2214
Fax: 1-800-730-2215
Web: http://www.thomsonrights.com

Thomson Wadsworth
10 Davis Drive
Belmont, CA 94002-3098
USA

Asia
Thomson Learning
5 Shenton Way #01-01
UIC Building
Singapore 068808

Australia/New Zealand
Thomson Learning
102 Dodds Street
Southbank, Victoria 3006
Australia

Canada
Nelson
1120 Birchmount Road
Toronto, Ontario M1K 5G4
Canada

Europe/Middle East/South Africa
Thomson Learning
High Holborn House
50/51 Bedford Row
London WC1R 4LR
United Kingdom

Latin America
Thomson Learning
Seneca, 53
Colonia Polanco
11560 Mexico D.F.
Mexico

Spain/Portugal
Paraninfo
Calle/Magallanes, 25
28015 Madrid, Spain

CONTENTS

Preface

We have developed this study guide to facilitate the learning process for you. The study guide includes a comprehensive collection of materials for each chapter to help you learn the subject matter covered by your instructor. Learning is a structured process and it is not a simple process. Each chapter includes learning objectives, key words with definitions, outlines, summaries, and chapter review questions consisting of multiple choice, true/false, fill in the blank, and essay. An answer key with page references is provided at the end of each chapter.

We have been teaching this material for over twenty years and we know how students learn this material best. The material is designed to help you get the most from your study time. You should love learning and you should enjoy the course material and your instructor. Preparing for class lectures and the exams with these materials should make those things happen. Good Luck!

Special thanks go to Sabra Horne and Jana Davis at Wadsworth Publishing for their support and assistance with this project. In addition, Sabra is to be commended for all of her support over the years to the promotion of great teaching in criminal justice higher education. Special thanks are also given to Dr. Elaine Rodney and Dr. Myrna Cintron of the College of Juvenile Justice and Psychology at Prairie View A&M University for their support and generosity that make being a scholar in criminal justice a great calling. Their support and generosity created the time to do this project, as well as the cooperative and peaceful climate which scholars need to pursue their dreams.

1 Crime and Criminology

LEARNING OBJECTIVES

After mastering the content of this chapter, a student should be able to:

1. Understand what is meant by the field of criminology.
2. Know the historical context of criminology.
3. Recognize the differences between the various schools of criminological thought.
4. Understand the various elements of the criminological enterprise.
5. Discuss how criminologists define crime.
6. Recognize the concepts of criminal law.
7. Show how the criminal law is undergoing change.
8. Discuss ethical issues in criminology.

KEY WORDS AND DEFINITIONS

Criminology - The scientific study of the nature, extent, cause, and control of criminal behavior.

Interdisciplinary - Involving two or more academic fields.

Utilitarianism - The view that people's behavior is motivated by the pursuit of pleasure and the avoidance of pain.

Classical criminology - The theoretical perspective suggesting that (1) people have free will to choose criminal or conventional behaviors; (2) people choose to commit crime for reasons of greed or personal need; and (3) crime can be controlled only by the fear of criminal sanctions.

Positivism - The branch of social science that uses the scientific method of the natural sciences and suggests that human behavior is a product of social, biological, psychological, or economic forces.

Biosocial theory - Approach to criminology that focuses on the interaction between biological and social factors as they relate to crime.

Sociological criminology - Approach to criminology, based on the work of Quertelet and Durkheim that focuses on the relationship between social factors and crime.

Anomie - A lack of norms or clear social standards. Because of rapidly shifting moral values, the individual has few guides to what is socially acceptable.

Chicago School - Group of urban sociologists who studied the relationship between environmental conditions and crime.

Socialization - Process of human development and enculturation. Socialization is influenced by key social processes and institutions.

Conflict theory - The view that human behavior is shaped by interpersonal conflict and that those who maintain social power will use it to further their own ends.

✳ Rational choice theory - The view that crime is a function of a decision-making process in which the potential offender weighs the potential costs and benefits of an illegal act.

✳ Social structure theory - The view that disadvantaged economic class position is a primary cause of crime.

Valid - Actually measuring what one intends to measure; relevant.

Reliable - Producing consistent results from one measurement to another.

Ex post facto law - A law applied retroactively to punish acts that were not crimes before its passage, or that raises the grade of an offense, or that renders an act punishable in a more severe manner than it was when committed.

White-collar crime - Illegal acts that capitalize on a person's status in the marketplace. White-collar crimes may include theft, embezzlement, fraud, market manipulation, restraint of trade, and false advertising.

✳ Penology - Subarea of criminology that focuses on the correction and control of criminal offenders.

Rehabilitation - Treatment of criminal offenders aimed at preventing future criminal behavior.

Capital punishment - The execution of criminal offenders; the death penalty.

Mandatory sentences - A statutory requirement that a certain penalty shall be carried out in all cases of conviction for a specified offense or series of offenses.

✳ Victimology - The study of the victim's role in criminal events.

✳ Deviance - Behavior that departs from the social norm but is not necessarily criminal.

Crime - An act, deemed socially harmful or dangerous, that is specifically defined, prohibited, and punished under the criminal law.

✳ Consensus view - The belief that the majority of citizens in a society share common values and agree on what behaviors should be defined as criminal.

Criminal law - The written code that defines crimes and their punishments.

✳ Conflict view - The belief that criminal behavior is defined by those in a position of power to protect and advance their own self-interest.

✳ Interactionist view - The belief that those with social power are able to impose their values on society as a whole, and these values then define criminal behavior.

Code of Hammurabi - The first written criminal code, developed in Babylonia about 2000 B.C.

Mosaic Code - The laws of the ancient Israelites, found in the Old Testament of the Judeo-Christian Bible.

Precedent - A rule derived from previous judicial decisions and applied to future cases; the basis of common law.

Common law - Early English law, developed by judges, which became the standardized law of the land in England and eventually formed the basis of the criminal law in the United States.

Statutory crimes - Crimes defined by legislative bodies in response to changing social conditions, public opinion, and custom.

Felony - A serious offense that carries a penalty of imprisonment, usually for one year or more, and may entail loss of political rights.

Misdemeanor - A minor crime usually punished by a short jail term and/or a fine.

Appellate court - Court that reviews trial court procedures to determine whether they have complied with accepted rules and constitutional doctrines.

Sampling - Selecting a limited number of people for study as representative of a larger group.

Population - All people who share a particular characteristic, such as all high school students or all police officers.

Cross-sectional research - Interviewing or questioning a diverse sample of subjects, representing a cross section of a community, at the same point in time.

Longitudinal research - Tracking the development of the same group of subjects over time.

Cohort - A group of subjects that is studied over time.

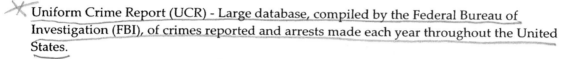
Uniform Crime Report (UCR) - Large database, compiled by the Federal Bureau of Investigation (FBI), of crimes reported and arrests made each year throughout the United States.

Experimental research - Manipulating or intervening in the lives of subjects to observe the outcome or effect of a specific intervention. True experiments usually include (1) random selection of subjects, (2) a control or comparison group, and (3) an experimental condition.

CHAPTER SUMMARY

Criminology is the scientific approach to the study of criminal behavior and society's reaction to law violations and violators. It is essentially an interdisciplinary field; many of its practitioners were originally trained as sociologists, psychologists, economists, political scientists, historians, and natural scientists. Criminology has a rich history, with roots in the utilitarian philosophy of Beccaria, the biological positivism of Lombroso, the social theory of Durkheim, and the political philosophy of Marx. The criminological enterprise includes subareas such as criminal statistics, the sociology of law, theory construction, criminal behavior systems, penology, and victimology.

When they define crime, criminologists typically hold one of three perspectives: the consensus view, the conflict view, or the interactionist view. The consensus view holds that criminal behavior is defined by laws that reflect the values and morals of a majority of citizens. The conflict view states that criminal behavior is defined in such a way that economically powerful groups can retain their control over society. The interactionist view portrays criminal behavior as a relativistic, constantly changing concept that reflects society's current moral values. According to the interactionist view, behavior is labeled as criminal by those in power; criminals are people society chooses to label as outsiders or deviants.

The criminal law is a set of rules that specify the behaviors society has outlawed. The criminal law serves several important purposes: It represents public opinion and moral values, it enforces social controls, it deters criminal behavior and wrongdoing, it punishes transgressors, it creates equity, and it banishes private retribution. The criminal law used in U.S. jurisdictions traces its origin to the English common law. In the U.S. legal system, lawmakers have codified common-law crimes into state and federal penal codes. The criminal law is undergoing constant reform. Some acts are being decriminalized—their penalties are being reduced—while penalties for others are becoming more severe.

Criminologists use various research methods to gather information that will shed light on criminal behavior. These methods include surveys, longitudinal studies, record studies, experiments, and observations. Ethical issues arise when information-gathering methods appear biased or exclusionary. These issues may cause serious consequences because research findings can significantly impact individuals and groups.

CHAPTER OUTLINE

I. A Brief History of Criminology
    A. Classical Criminology
    B. Positivist Criminology
    C. Sociological Criminology
    D. Conflict Criminology
    E. Contemporary Criminology

II. What Criminologists Do: The Field of Criminology
    A. Criminal Statistics/Crime Measurement
    B. RACE, CULTURE, GENDER AND CRIMINOLOGY
        1. International Crime Trends
    C. Sociology of Law
    D. Developing Theories of Crime Causation
    E. Understanding and Describing Criminal Behavior
    F. Penology
    G. Victimology

III. Deviant or Criminal? How Criminologists Define Crime
    A. The Consensus View of Crime
    B. The Conflict View of Crime
    C. The Interactionist View of Crime
    D. A Definition of Crime

IV. Crime and the Criminal Law
    A. Common Law
    B. Contemporary Criminal Law
    C. The Evolution of Criminal Law

V. Criminological Research Methods
    A. Survey Research
    B. Cohort Research
    C. Record Data Analysis
    D. Experimental Research
    E. Observational and Interview Research

VI. Ethical Issues in Criminology

CHAPTER REVIEW QUESTIONS

Multiple Choice

1. Criminology is _____ science.
    a. a unidisciplinary
    b. an interdisciplinary
    c. a pure
    d. primarily a psychological

2. Lombroso's early scientific work was called _____.
    a. atavism
    b. biological determinism
    c. biosocial theory
    d. none of the above

3. The scientific method is a main element of _____.
    a. Classical Criminology
    b. Utilitarianism
    c. Positivism
    d. Atavism
    e. all of the above

4. Norm and role confusion resulting from structural changes in society is called _____ by Durkheim.
    a. anomie
    b. atavism
    c. phrenology
    d. penology
    e. none of the above

5. Quertelet and Durkheim were the pioneering founders of _____ criminology.
    a. biological
    b. sociological
    c. classical
    d. positivist
    e. none of the above

6. Sutherland linked criminality to the failure of _____.
    a. socialization,
    b. schools
    c. caregivers
    d. churches
    e. all of the above

7. The view that human behavior is shaped by interpersonal conflict and that those in power will use it to further their own ends is _____.
   a. Positivism
   b. Socialization
   c. Classical
   d. Conflict
   e. none of the above

8. Which type of research involves studying people at the same point in time?
   a. cross-sectional
   b. longitudinal
   c. cohort
   d. b and c only

9. Which type of research involves tracking the development of the same group of subjects over time?
   a. cross-sectional
   b. longitudinal
   c. cohort
   d. b and c only

10. Crimes are behaviors that all elements of society consider to be repugnant according to _____.
    a. the consensus view of crime
    b. the conflict view of crime
    c. the interactionist view of crime
    d. none of the above

11. According to which view of crime does the definition of crime reflect the preferences and opinions of people who hold social power in a particular legal jurisdiction?
    a. the consensus view of crime
    b. the conflict view of crime
    c. the interactionist view of crime
    d. none of the above

12. Which view of crime depicts society as a collection of diverse groups who are in constant and continuing conflict?
    a. the consensus view of crime
    b. the conflict view of crime
    c. the interactionist view of crime
    d. none of the above

13. The academic discipline of criminology uses scientific methods to study the_____ of criminal behavior.
    a. nature
    b. extent
    c. cause
    d. control
    e. all of the above
    f. none of the above

14. Positivist criminology is the application of _____ to the study of human behavior.
    a. the scientific method
    b. humanism
    c. utilitarianism
    d. hedonism

15. The most commonly represented discipline in criminology is _____.
    a. political science
    b. sociology
    c. criminal justice
    d. psychology
    e. none of the above

16. What type of crime measure measures what one intends to measure?
    a. valid
    b. reliable
    c. official
    d. unofficial

17. Karl Marx discussed how crime is caused by _____.
    a. socialism
    b. communism
    c. capitalism
    d. none of the above

18. The major ethical issues in the study of crime and criminality include _____.
    a. what to study
    b. whom to study
    c. how to study
    d. all of the above
    e. none of the above.

19. When defining crime, criminologists typically hold which of the following perspectives?
    a. the consensus view
    b. the conflict view
    c. the interactionist view
    d. all of the above
    e. none of the above

20. The roots of criminology come from _____.
    a. the utilitarian philosophy of Beccaria
    b. the biological positivism of Lombroso
    c. the social theory of Durkheim
    d. the political philosophy of Marx
    e. all of the above

True/False

1. T / F For punishment to be effective, it must be public, prompt, necessary, the least possible in the given circumstances, proportionate, and dictated by law.

7

2. T /(F) The "father of criminology" was August Comte.

3. (T)/ F Positivists would challenge a concept such as the "soul" because it cannot be verified by the scientific method.

4. T /(F) Positivists believe that deviant behavior is a product of free will of the individual.

5. T / F The consensus view claims the law is a tool of the ruling class.

6. T /(F) Statutory crimes are also known as mala in se crimes.

7. (T)/ F The Mosaic Code contains the laws of the ancient Israelites, found in the Old Testament of the Judeo-Christian Bible.

8. (T)/ F Classical criminology suggests that people choose to commit crime for reasons of greed or personal need.

9. T /(F) The Chicago School sociologists argued that crime was a function of personal traits or characteristics.

10. (T)/ F Social structure theory is the view that disadvantaged economic class position is a primary cause of crime.

11. (T)/ F Theory construction is the process of predicting individual behavior.

12. (T)/ F An accurate measurement of crime must be valid.

13. (T)/ F The Enron scandal is an example of white-collar crime.

14. T /(F) Retribution involves the treatment of criminal offenders aimed at preventing future criminal behavior.

15. (T)/ F The purpose of equity in the criminal law is to make criminals pay back for their crimes.

Fill in the Blank

1. Criminology is an academic discipline that uses scientific methods to study the _Cause_ , _extent_ , _nature_ , and _Control_ of criminal behavior.

2. Social philosophers in the mid-eighteenth century wanted a more _rational_ approach to punishment.

3. The catch phrase of the classical perspective was _let the punishment fit the crime_

4. Positivist criminology is the application of _scientific method_ to the study of human behavior.

5. According to Durkheim, crime is _normal_ because it is virtually impossible to imagine a society without it.

6. Classical theory has evolved into modern _rational choice theory_

7. Deviance is behavior that departs from the social norm but is not necessarily _crime_ .

8. The written code that defines crimes and their punishments is known as
   law (criminal)

9. Mala prohibitum crimes are also known as _statutory_ crimes

10. A _misdemeanor_ is a minor crime usually punished by a short jail term and/or a fine.

11. _appellate_ courts review trial court procedures to determine whether they have complied with accepted rules and constitutional doctrines.

12. Criminology is a(n) _interdisciplinary_ science.

13. _Utilitarionism_ is the view that people's behavior is motivated by the pursuit of pleasure and the avoidance of pain.

14. _Social structure theory_ is the view that disadvantaged economic class position is a primary cause of crime.

15. _penology_ involves the correction and control of known criminal offenders.

Essay

1. Discuss the basic elements of classical criminology.

   1) People have free will to choose lawful or unlawful solutions to meet their needs or solve their problems.
   2) Unlawful actions may be more appealing as they are less work for greater reward
   3) Crime can be controlled by a person's fear of punishment.
   4) Punishment should be swift, severe, & certain to control crime.

2. Discuss the two main elements of Positivism.

   1) External forces (ie social status, wealth or even biological make up) that are beyond a Person's control influence human behaviors.
   2) They rely on the scientific method. They argue intelligence exists because it can be measured, but how do we know the soul exists as it can not.

3. Discuss Durkheim's idea that as societal structure changes, anomie results, and crime occurs.

4. Discuss the evolution of contemporary criminology.

5. Discuss the purposes of the criminal law.

ANSWER KEY FOR CHAPTER REVIEW QUESTIONS

Multiple Choice

1.	(b) an interdisciplinary	p. 3
2.	(b) biological determinism	p. 6
3.	(c) Positivism	p. 5
4.	(a) anomie	p. 6
5.	(b) sociological	p. 6
6.	(e) all of the above	p. 7
7.	(d) Conflict	p. 7
8.	(a) cross-sectional	p. 19
9.	(d) b and c only	p. 19
10.	(a) the consensus view of crime	p. 14
11.	(c) the interactionist view of crime	p. 14
12.	(b) the conflict view of crime	p. 14
13.	(e) all of the above	p. 3
14.	(a) the scientific method	p. 4
15.	(b) sociology	p. 3
16.	(a) valid	p. 10
17.	(c) capitalism	p. 7
18.	(d) all of the above	p. 22
19.	(d) all of the above	p. 23
20.	(e) all of the above	p. 23

True/False

1.	True	p. 4
2.	False	p. 6
3.	True	p. 5
4.	False	p. 5
5.	False	p. 15
6.	False	p. 16
7.	True	p. 16
8.	True	p. 4
9.	False	p. 7
10.	True	p. 8
11.	True	p. 9
12.	True	p. 10
13.	True	p. 12
14.	False	p. 13
15.	True	p. 17

Fill In the Blank

1. nature, extent, cause, and control   p. 3
2. rational   p. 4
3. "let the punishment fit the crime"   p. 4
4. the scientific method   p. 4
5. normal   p. 6
6. rational choice theory   p. 8
7. criminal   p. 13
8. the criminal law   p. 14
9. statutory crimes   p. 16
10. misdemeanor   p. 17
11. appellate   p. 18
12. interdisciplinary   p. 3
13. utilitarianism   p. 4
14. social structure theory   p. 8
15. penology   p. 13

Essay

1. p. 4
2. p. 5
3. pp. 6-7
4. p. 8
5. pp.17-8

2 The Nature and Extent of Crime

LEARNING OBJECTIVES

After mastering the content of this chapter, a student should be able to:

1. Become familiar with the various forms of crime data.
2. Understand the problems associated with collecting valid crime data.
3. Discuss the recent trends in the crime rate.
4. Identify the factors that influence crime rates.
5. Understand the patterns in the crime rate.
6. Recognize age, gender, and racial patterns in crime.
7. Discuss the association between social class and crime.
8. Describe the various positions on gun control.
9. Understand Wolfgang's pioneering research on chronic offending.
10. Understand the influence the discovery of the chronic offender has had on criminology.

KEY WORDS AND DEFINITIONS

Uniform Crime Report (UCR) - Large database, compiled by the Federal Bureau of Investigation (FBI), of crimes reported and arrests made each year throughout the United States.

Index crimes - The eight most serious offenses included in the UCR: murder, rape, assault, robbery, burglary, arson, larceny, and motor vehicle theft.

National Crime Victimization Survey (NCVS) - The ongoing victimization study conducted jointly by the Justice Department and the U.S. Census Bureau that surveys victims about their experiences with law violation.

Self-report surveys - A research approach that requires subjects to reveal their own participation delinquent or criminal acts.

Instrumental crimes - Offenses designed to improve the financial or social position of the criminal.

Expressive crimes - Offenses committed not for profit or gain but to vent rage, anger, or frustration.

Aging out (desistance) - The fact that people commit less crime as they mature.

Masculinity hypothesis - The view that women who commit crimes have biological and psychological traits similar to those of men.

Racial threat view - As the size of the black population increases, the perceived threat to the white population increases, resulting in a greater amount of social control imposed against blacks.

Chronic offenders - A small group of persistent offenders who account for a majority of all criminal offenses.

CHAPTER SUMMARY

The three primary sources of crime statistics are the Uniform Crime Reports, based on police data accumulated by the FBI; self-reports from criminal behavior surveys; and victim surveys. Each data source has its strengths and weaknesses, and, although quite different from one another, they actually agree on the nature of criminal behavior. The crime data indicate that rates have declined significantly in the past few years and are now far less than they were a decade ago. Suspected causes for the crime rate drop include an increasing prison population, more cops of the street, the end of the crack epidemic, the availability of abortion, and the age structure of society. The data sources show stable patterns in the crime rate. Ecological patterns show that crime varies by season and by urban versus rural environment.

There is also evidence of gender patterns in the crime rate: Men commit more crime than women. Age influences crime. Young people commit more crime than the elderly. Crime data show that people commit less crime as they age, but the significance and cause of this pattern are still not completely understood. Similarly, racial and class patterns appear in the crime rate. However, it is still unclear whether these are true differences or a function of discriminatory law enforcement.

One of the most important findings in the crime statistics is the existence of the chronic offender, a repeat criminal responsible for a significant amount of all law violations. Chronic offenders begin their careers early in life and, rather than aging out of crime, persist into adulthood.

CHAPTER OUTLINE

   I.   The Uniform Crime Report
       A.   Validity of the UCR
       B.   The National Incident-Based Reporting System
  II.   Victim Surveys
       A.   NCVS Findings
       B.   Validity of the NCVS
 III.   Self-Report Surveys
       A.   Accuracy of Self-Reports
 IV.   Evaluating Crime Data
   V.   Crime Trends
       A.   CURRENT ISSUES IN CRIME
           1.   Explaining Crime Trends
       B.   Trends in Violent Crime
       C.   Trends in Property Crime
       D.   Trends in Self-Reports and Victimization
       E.   What the Future Holds
 VI.   Crime Patterns
       A.   The Ecology of Crime
       B.   Use of Firearms

CHAPTER REVIEW QUESTIONS

Multiple Choice

1. The relationship between guns and _____ may influence the crime rate.
    a. the economy
    b. age
    c. social malaise
    d. abortion
    e. none of the above

2. The property crimes reported in the UCR do not include _____.
    a. larceny
    b. motor vehicle theft
    c. arson
    d. robbery

3. According to the _____, male crime rates are much higher than those of females.
    a. UCR
    b. self-report data
    c. victimization surveys
    d. all of the above

4. Explanations for the relationship between gender and crime include _____.
    a. trait differences
    b. socialization differences
    c. feminist views
    d. all of the above

5. The perception that racial discrimination is part of the arrest process is supported by the _____.
    a. UCR
    b. self-report data
    c. victimization data
    d. all of the above

6. Crime is more common in the _____.
    a. fall
    b. winter
    c. spring
    d. summer

15

7. Crime is more likely to occur in _____.
   a. rural areas
   b. urban areas
   c. both rural and urban areas
   d. none of the above

8. According to _____, crime rates are highest in areas with high rates of poverty.
   a. the UCR
   b. self-report data
   c. victimization data
   d. none of the above

9. Persistent offenders are referred to as _____.
   a. career criminals
   b. chronic offenders
   c. majority offenders
   d. petty offenders
   e. a and b only
   f. c and d only

10. The UCR contains arrest data for _____.
    a. cities
    b. counties
    c. SMSA's
    d. geographical divisions of the United States
    e. all of the above

11. The reason why some people may not report crime to the police is because _____.
    a. they may believe victimization is a private matter
    b. nothing could be done
    c. the victimization was not important enough
    d. they do not trust the police
    e. all of the above

12. Over-reporting of criminal victimization in victim surveys results from _____.
    a. the embarrassment of reporting the crime to the interviewer
    b. sampling error
    c. inadequate question format
    d. the victims' misinterpretation of events

13. The basic assumption of self-report studies is _____.
    a. accurate victimization rates
    b. the most valid official data possible
    c. their inaccuracy
    d. the assurance of anonymity and confidentiality

14. Which data source remains the standard unit of analysis upon which most criminological research is based?
    a. the UCR
    b. self-report data
    c. victimization data
    d. all of the above

15. What methods are used to express crime data in the UCR?
    a. raw figures
    b. crime rates
    c. changes over time
    d. all of the above
    e. none of the above

16. The unlawful entry of a structure to commit a felony or a theft is the crime of _____. Attempted forcible entry is included.
    a. aggravated assault
    b. robbery
    c. burglary
    d. theft
    e. none of the above

17. The National Crime Victimization Survey (NCVS) is conducted by _____.
    a. the FBI
    b. the Justice Department
    c. the U.S. Census Bureau
    d. a only
    e. b and c only

18. Which crime sources are not official crime data?
    a. the UCR
    b. the NCVS
    c. self-Report surveys
    d. a and c only
    e. b and c only

19. The NCVS samples more than _____ annually to estimate crime victimization.
    a. 10,000
    b. 50,000
    c. 100,000
    d. 500,000

20. Crime rates peaked in _____.
    a. 1975
    b. the 1980s
    c. 1985
    d. the 1990s

True/False

1. T / F The availability of firearms may influence the crime rate, especially the proliferation of weapons in the hands of teens.

2. T / F One factor that affects crime rates is the explosive growth in teenage gangs.

3. T / F The recent decrease in property crimes has been more dramatic than the decrease in violent crime.

4. T / F The murder statistics are regarded as the most accurate aspect of the UCR.

5. T / F The UCR appears to be more stable than self-report results.

6. T / F All experts agree that crime rates will increase in the future.

7. T / F Selling narcotics is an example of an expressive crime.

8. T / F Rape and assault are examples of expressive crimes.

9. T / F Drug use is an example of an instrumental crime.

10. T / F Younger people commit crime more often than their older peers.

11. T / F Males commit more crimes than females.

12. T / F Female crime rates have been declining.

13. T / F Crime is more likely to occur in rural areas.

14. T / F A small group of persistent offenders accounts for a majority of all criminal offenses.

15. T / F The UCR, self-report data, and victimization data actually agree on the nature of criminal behavior.

Fill in the Blank

1. The FBI's _____ is an annual tally of crime reported to local police departments.

2. _____ ask respondents about their own criminal activity.

3. Some experts tie increases in the violent crime rate between 1980 and 1990 to the _____.

4. _____ has had a significant impact on murder rates.

5. Violent victimization rates have declined since _____, reaching the lowest level ever recorded in _____.

6. Robbery rates increase in the winter partly because of _____.

7. The proliferation of _____ and the high rate of lethal violence they cause is the single most significant factor separating the crime problem in the United States from the rest of the developing world.

8. _____ crimes are offenses designed to improve the financial or social position of the criminal.

9. _____ crimes are offenses committed not for profit or gain but to vent rage, anger, or frustration.

10. The fact that people commit less crime as they mature is referred to as _____.

11. When a person does not age out of crime, the person is pursuing a _____.

12. The number of crimes committed per 100,000 people is known as the _____.

13. No _____ crimes are reported in the UCR which affects its validity.

14. _____ crimes often go undetected.

15. Most self-report surveys have focused on _____.

Essay

1. Discuss the factors believed to influence the crime rate.

2. Why does aging out occur?

3. Discuss the chronic offender and what it means for understanding criminality.

4. Compare the UCR, self-reports, and victimization surveys.

5. Discuss the relationship between race and crime.

ANSWER KEY FOR CHAPTER REVIEW QUESTIONS

Multiple Choice

1.	(b) Age	p. 34
2.	(d) Robbery	p. 36
3.	(d) all of the above	p. 45
4.	(d) all of the above	p. 45
5.	(b) self-report data	p. 46
6.	(d) summer	p. 47
7.	(b) urban areas	p. 47
8.	(a) The UCR	p. 47
9.	(e) a and b only	p. 47
10.	(e) all of the above	p. 28
11.	(e) all of the above	p. 29
12.	(d) the victim's misinterpretation of events	p. 31
13.	(d) the assurance of anonymity and confidentiality	p. 31
14.	(a) The UCR	p. 32
15.	(d) all of the above	pp. 28-29
16.	(c) burglary	p. 28
17.	(e) b and c only	p. 30
18.	(e) b and c only	p. 31
19.	(b) 50,000	p. 38
20.	(d) the 1990s	p. 38

True/False

1.	True	p. 34
2.	True	p. 35
3.	False	p. 36
4.	True	p. 36
5.	False	p. 37
6.	False	p. 38
7.	False	p. 40
8.	True	p. 40
9.	False	p. 40
10.	True	p. 44
11.	True	p. 45
12.	False	p. 45
13.	False	p. 47
14.	True	p. 47
15.	True	p. 48

Fill in the Blank

1.	Uniform Crime Report	p. 38
2.	Self-report surveys	p. 38
3.	crack epidemic	p. 35
4.	Medical technology	p. 35
5.	1994; 2002	p. 39
6.	the Christmas shopping season	p. 40
7.	handguns	p. 40
8.	Instrumental	p. 40
9.	Expressive	p. 40
10.	acting out or desistance	p. 44
11.	criminal career	p. 44
12.	crime rate	p. 28
13.	federal	p. 29
14.	Victimless	p. 29
15.	juveniles	p. 31

Essay

1. pp. 34-5
2. p. 44
3. pp. 47-8
4. pp. 28-32
5. pp. 46-7

3 Victims and Victimization

LEARNING OBJECTIVES

After mastering the content of this chapter, a student should be able to:

1. Understand the concept of victimization.
2. Describe the nature of victimization.
3. Discuss the problems of crime victims.
4. Understand the costs of victimization.
5. Discuss the relationship between victimization and antisocial behavior.
6. Recognize the age, gender, and racial patterns in victimization data.
7. Discuss the association between lifestyle and victimization.
8. Understand the term victim precipitation.
9. List the routine activities associated with victimization risk.
10. Discuss the various victim assistance programs.

KEY WORDS AND DEFINITIONS

Victimology - The study of the victim's role in criminal events.

Victimologists - Criminologists who focus on the victims of crime.

Posttraumatic stress disorder - Psychological reaction to a highly stressful event; symptoms may include depression, anxiety, flashbacks, and recurring nightmares.

Cycle of violence - Victims of crime, especially childhood abuse, are more likely to commit crimes themselves.

Victim precipitation theory - The view that victims may initiate, either actively or passively, the confrontation that leads to their victimization.

Active precipitation - Aggressive or provocative behavior of victims that results in their victimization.

Passive precipitation - Personal or social characteristics of victims that make them "attractive" targets for criminals; such victims may unknowingly either threaten or encourage their attackers.

Lifestyle theories - The view that people become crime victims because of lifestyles that increase their exposure to criminal offenders.

Deviant place theory - The view that victimization is primarily a function of where people live.

Routine activities theory - The view that victimization results from the interaction of three everyday factors: the availability of suitable targets, the absence of capable guardians, and the presence of motivated offenders.

Suitable targets - Objects of crime (persons or property) that are attractive and readily available.

Capable guardians - Effective deterrents to crime, such as police or watchful neighbors.

Motivated offenders - People willing and able to commit crimes.

Victim–witness assistance programs - Government programs that help crime victims and witnesses; may include compensation, court services, and/or crisis intervention.

Compensation - Financial aid awarded to crime victims to repay them for their loss and injuries; may cover medical bills, loss of wages, loss of future earnings, and/or counseling.

Crisis intervention - Emergency counseling for crime victims.

Victim–offender reconciliation programs - Mediated face-to-face encounters between victims and their attackers, designed to produce restitution agreements and, if possible, reconciliation.

CHAPTER SUMMARY

Criminologists now consider victims and victimization a major focus of study. About 23 million U.S. citizens are victims of crime each year. Like the crime rate, the victimization rate has been in sharp decline. The social and economic costs of crime are in the billions of dollars annually. Victims suffer long-term consequences such as experiencing fear and posttraumatic stress disorder. Research shows that victims are more likely than nonvictims to engage in antisocial behavior.

Like crime, victimization has stable patterns and trends. Violent crime victims tend to be young, poor, single males living in large cities, although victims come in all ages, sizes, races, and genders. Females are more likely than males to be victimized by somebody they know. Adolescents maintain a high risk of being physically and sexually victimized. Their victimization has been linked to a multitude of subsequent social problems. Many victimizations occur in the home, and many victims are the target of relatives and loved ones.

There are a number of theories of victimization (see Concept Summary 3.1). One view, called victim precipitation, is that victims provoke criminals. Lifestyle theories suggest that victims put themselves in danger by engaging in high-risk activities, such as going out late at night, living in a high-crime area, and associating with high-risk peers. Deviant place theory argues that victimization risk is related to neighborhood crime rates. The routine activities theory maintains that a pool of motivated offenders exists and that these offenders will take advantage of unguarded, suitable targets. Numerous programs help victims by providing court services, economic compensation, public education, and crisis intervention. Most states have created a Victims' Bill of Rights.

CHAPTER OUTLINE

I. The Victim's Role

II. Problems of Crime Victims

    A. Economic Loss

    B. System Abuse

    C. Long-Term Stress

    D. Fear

    E. Antisocial Behavior

III. The Nature of Victimization

CHAPTER REVIEW QUESTIONS

Multiple Choice

1. The scientific study of victims is called _____.
   a. criminology
   b. victimology
   c. forensics
   d. psychology

2. The long-term stress associated with crime victimization resulting in depression, anxiety, flashbacks, and recurring nightmares is called _____.
   a. posttraumatic stress disorder
   b. disassociation
   c. psychosis
   d. victimization anxiety

3. Research shows that _____ are more likely to engage in violent behavior if they were the target of physical abuse and were exposed to violent behavior among adults they know or live with, or exposed to weapons.
   a. boys
   b. girls
   c. both boys and girls
   d. toddlers

4. Victimization is not random but a function of _____ factors.
   a. educational
   b. personal
   c. institutional
   d. ecological
   e. b and d only

5. The more serious violent crimes, such as rape and aggravated assault, typically take place _____.
   a. during the daytime
   b. in the early morning hours
   c. after 6 P.M.
   d. in the late afternoon hours

6. Those living in the central city have significantly _____ rates of theft and violence in comparison to suburbanites.
   a. higher
   b. lower
   c. similar
   d. dissimilar

7. Which types of homes are the most vulnerable to crime?
   a. smaller
   b. African American
   c. Eastern
   d. rural

8. The most important factor(s) distinguishing victims from nonvictims include _____.
   a. gender
   b. type of job
   c. number of people in household
   d. none of the above

9. Victim risk diminished rapidly after age _____.
   a. 25
   b. 30
   c. 35
   d. 40
   e. 45

10. People over age 65 account for about _____ percent of violent victimization.
    a. 1
    b. 4
    c. 10
    d. 15

11. According to victim precipitation theory, which type of precipitation occurs when victims act provocatively, use threats or fighting words, or even attack first?
    a. active
    b. passive
    c. lifestyle
    d. routine

12. The victim's characteristics of physical weakness or psychological distress that renders them incapable of resisting or deterring crime and makes them easy targets are called _____ factors.
    a. target vulnerability
    b. target gratifiability
    c. target antagonism
    d. target hostility

13. The victim's characteristics that include having attractive possesses are called _____ factors.
    a. target vulnerability
    b. target gratifiability
    c. target antagonism
    d. target hostility

14. The victim's characteristics that arouse anger, jealousy, or destructive impulses are called _____ factors.
    a. target vulnerability
    b. target gratifiability
    c. target antagonism
    d. target hostility

15. Victims report that substance abuse was involved in about _____ of violent crimes.
    a. 25%
    b. 33%
    c. 50%
    d. 75%

16. According to the _____ theory, victims do not encourage crime, but are victim prone because they reside in socially disorganized high-crime areas where they have the greatest risk of coming into contact with criminal offenders, irrespective of their own behavior or lifestyle.
    a. lifestyle
    b. victim precipitation
    c. routine activities
    d. deviant place

17. Routine activities theory examines the interaction of three variables that reflect the routine activities of the typical American lifestyle. Which of the following is not one of those variables?
    a. availability of suitable targets
    b. absence of capable guardians
    c. absence of suitable targets
    d. presence of motivated offenders

18. National victim surveys indicate that almost every American age _____ and over will one day become the victim of common-law crimes, such as larceny and burglary.
    a. 12
    b. 16
    c. 18
    d. 21

19. Surveys show that over _____ percent of the general public have been victimized by crime at least once in their lives.
    a. 25
    b. 50
    c. 75
    d. 90

20. An estimated _____ victim witness assistance programs have been developed throughout the United States.
    a. 2,000
    b. 20,000
    c. 200,000
    d. 350,000

True/False

1. T / F Research shows that both boys and girls are more likely to engage in violent behavior if they were the target of physical abuse or were exposed to violent behavior among adults they know or live with, or exposed to weapons.

2. T / F The long-term stress associated with crime victimization resulting in depression, anxiety, flashbacks, and recurring nightmares is called victimization anxiety.

3. T / F The more serious violent crimes, such as rape and aggravated assault, typically take place during the daytime.

4. T / F Less serious forms of violence, such as unarmed robberies and personal larcenies like purse snatching, are more likely to occur during the daytime.

5. T / F Rural, European-American homes in the Northeast are the least likely to be vulnerable to crime.

6. T / F Renters are less vulnerable to crimes than people who own their own homes.

7. T / F Females are more likely than males to be the victims of violent crime.

8. T / F Men are almost twice as likely as women to experience robbery.

9. T / F Gender differences in the victimization rate appear to be increasing.

10. T / F Females are most often victimized by someone they knew.

11. T / F Households that have experienced victimization in the past are the ones most likely to experience it again in the future.

12. T / F Capable guardians include teenage boys.

13. T / F Suitable targets for crime include unlocked homes.

14. T / F Less than half of all victim programs include public education.

15. T / F Most victim programs refer victims to specific services to help them recover from their ordeal.

Fill in the Blank

1. Scholars who focus their attention on crime victims are called _____.

2. The cost of crime victimization is estimated to be in the hundreds of _____ of dollars.

3. There is growing evidence that crime victims are _____ likely to commit crimes themselves.

4. People, especially young _____, who are physically or sexually abused, are much more likely to smoke, drink, and take drugs than are non-abused youth.

5. Some people and places are targets of _____ victimization.

6. Crime victimization tends to be _____ racial.

7. Women were _____ likely than men to be robbed by a friend or acquaintance.

8. A study on sexual victimization by Fisher and her colleagues found that _____ percent of the victims knew the person who sexually victimized them.

9. _____ precipitation occurs when the victim exhibits some personal characteristic that unknowingly either threatens or encourages the attacker.

10. Some people live in places that are magnets for _____.

11. Some experts link victimization to _____ lifestyles.

12. One of the primary goals of victim advocates has been to lobby for legislation creating crime victim _____ programs.

13. Emergency counseling for victims is called _____.

14. Victim-Offender Reconciliation Programs use _____ to facilitate face-to-face encounters between victims and their attackers.

15. Most jurisdictions allow victims to make a _____ before the sentencing judge.

Essay

1. Explain potential reasons for the decline in household victimization rates during the last fifteen years.

2. Discuss the interaction of three variables that reflect the routine activities of the typical American lifestyle and the relationship of those variables to victimization.

3. Discuss Deviant Place Theory and the role of place in victimization risk.

4. Discuss posttraumatic stress disorder and how it can result from crime victimization.

5. Discuss the general rights included in most states' Victims' Bill of Rights.

ANSWER KEY FOR CHAPTER REVIEW QUESTIONS

Multiple Choice

1.	(b) victimology	p. 52
2.	(a) posttraumatic stress disorder	p. 53
3.	(c) both boys and girls	p. 54
4.	(e) b and d only	p. 55
5.	(c) after 6 P.M.	p. 55
6.	(a) higher	p. 55
7.	(b) African-American	p. 56
8.	(a) gender	p. 56
9.	(a) 25	p. 57
10.	(a) 1%	p. 57
11.	(a) active	p. 59
12.	(a) target vulnerability	p. 58
13.	(b) target gratifiability	pp. 58-59
14.	(c) target antagonism	p. 59
15.	(b) 33%	p. 59
16.	(d) deviant place	p. 62
17.	(c) absence of suitable targets	p. 62
18.	(a) 12	p. 64
19.	(c) 75	p. 64
20.	(a) 2,000	p. 65

True/False

1.	False	p. 54
2.	False	p. 53
3.	False	p. 55
4.	True	p. 55
5.	True	p. 56
6.	False	p. 56
7.	False	p. 56
8.	True	p. 56
9.	False	p. 56
10.	True	p. 56
11.	True	p. 58
12.	False	p. 63
13.	True	p. 63
14.	False	p. 66
15.	True	p. 66

Fill in the Blank

1.	victimologists	p. 52
2.	billions	p. 52
3.	more	p. 54
4.	males	p. 54
5.	repeat	p. 59
6.	intra	p. 59
7.	more	p. 59
8.	90%	p. 61
9.	Passive	p. 60
10.	criminals	p. 63
11.	high-risk	p. 63
12.	compensation	p. 65
13.	crisis intervention	p. 66
14.	mediators	pp. 66-67
15.	victim impact statement	p. 66

Essay

1. p. 56
2. p. 62
3. p. 62
4. p. 63
5. p. 67

4 Choice Theory: Because They Want To

LEARNING OBJECTIVES

After mastering the content of this chapter, a student should be able to:

1. Understand the concept of rational choice.
2. Know the work of Beccaria.
3. Discuss the concepts of offense and offender-specific crime.
4. Discuss why violent and drug crimes are rational.
5. Summarize the various techniques of situational crime prevention.
6. Discuss the association between punishment and crime.
7. Understand the concepts of certainty, severity, and speed of punishment.
8. Understand what is meant by specific deterrence.
9. Discuss the issues involving the use of incapacitation.
10. Understand the concept of "just desert."

KEY WORDS AND DEFINITIONS

Rational choice - The view that crime is a function of a decision-making process in which the potential offender weighs the potential costs and benefits of an illegal act.

Choice theory - The school of thought holding that people choose to engage in delinquent and criminal behavior after weighing the consequences and benefits of their actions.

Classical criminology - The theoretical perspective suggesting that (1) people have free will to choose criminal or conventional behaviors; (2) people choose to commit crime for reasons of greed or personal need; and (3) crime can be controlled only by the fear of criminal sanctions.

Offense-specific - The idea that offenders react selectively to the characteristics of particular crimes.

Offender-specific - The idea that offenders evaluate their skills, motives, needs, and fears before deciding to commit crime.

Edgework - The excitement or exhilaration of successfully executing illegal activities in dangerous situations.

Seductions of crime - The situational inducements or immediate benefits that draw offenders into law violations.

Situational crime prevention - A method of crime prevention that seeks to eliminate or reduce particular crimes in narrow settings.

Defensible space - The principle that crime can be prevented to reduce the opportunity individuals have to commit crime.

Displacement - An effect of crime prevention efforts in which efforts to control crime in one area shift illegal activities to another.

Extinction - The phenomenon in which a crime prevention effort has an immediate impact that then dissipates as criminals adjust to new conditions.

Diffusion of benefits - An effect that occurs when efforts to prevent one crime unintentionally prevent another, or when crime control efforts in one locale reduce crime in other nontarget areas.

Discouragement - An effect that occurs when limiting access to one target reduces other types of crime as well.

General deterrence - A crime control policy that depends on the fear of criminal penalties, convincing the potential law violator that the pains associated with crime outweigh its benefits.

Crackdown - The concentration of police resources a particular problem area to eradicate displace criminal activity.

Brutalization effect - The belief that capital punishment creates an atmosphere of brutality that enhances rather than deters the level of violence society.

Specific deterrence - The view that criminal sanctions should be so powerful that offenders will never repeat their criminal acts.

Incarceration - Confinement in jail or prison.

Recidivism - Repetition of criminal behavior.

Incapacitation effect - The idea that keeping offenders in confinement will eliminate the risk of their committing further offenses.

Three strikes and you're out - Policy whereby people convicted of three felony offenses receive a mandatory life sentence.

Just desert - The principle that those who violate the rights of others deserve punishment commensurate with the seriousness of the crime, without regard to their personal characteristics or circumstances.

CHAPTER SUMMARY

Choice theories assume that criminals carefully choose whether to commit criminal acts. These theories are summarized in Concept Summary 4.2. People are influenced by their fear of the criminal penalties associated with being caught and convicted for law violations. The choice approach is rooted in the classical criminology of Cesare Beccaria, who argued that punishment should be certain, swift, and severe enough to deter crime. Today, choice theorists view crime as offense- and offender-specific. Offense-specific means that the characteristics of the crime control whether it occurs. For example, carefully protecting a home makes it less likely to be a target of crime. Offender-specific refers to the personal characteristics of potential criminals. People with specific skills and needs may be more likely to commit crime than others.

Research shows that offenders consider their targets carefully before deciding on a course of action. Even violent criminals and drug addicts show signs of rationality. By implication, crime can be prevented or displaced by convincing potential criminals that the risks of violating the law exceed the benefits. Situational crime prevention is the application of security and protective devices that make it more difficult to commit crime or reduce criminal rewards.

Deterrence theory holds that if criminals are indeed rational, an inverse relationship should exist between punishment and crime. The certainty of punishment seems to deter crime. If people do not believe they will be caught, even harsh punishment may not deter crime. Deterrence theory has been criticized on the grounds that it wrongfully assumes that criminals make a rational choice before committing crimes, that it ignores the intricacies of the criminal justice system, and that it does not take into account the social and psychological factors that may influence criminality. A big disappointment for deterrence theory is the fact that the death penalty does not seem to reduce murders. Specific deterrence theory holds that the crime rate can be reduced if known offenders are punished so severely that they never commit crimes again.

There is little evidence that harsh punishment actually reduces the crime rate. Most prison inmates recidivate. Incapacitation theory maintains that if deterrence does not work, the best course of action is to incarcerate known offenders for long periods so that they lack criminal opportunity. Research efforts have not proved that increasing the number of people in prison—and increasing prison sentences —will reduce crime rates.

CHAPTER OUTLINE

I.   The Development of Rational Choice Theory

II. The Concepts of Rational Choice

   A.   Offense- and Offender-Specific Crime

   B.   Structuring Criminality

   C.   Structuring Crime

III. Is Crime Rational?

   A.   Are Street Crimes Rational?

   B.   Is Drug Use Rational?

   C.   Can Violence Be Rational?

IV. Why Do People Commit Crime?

   A.   CURRENT ISSUES IN CRIME

      1.   Can Crime Pay Dividends?

V.   Preventing Crime

   A.   Crime Prevention Strategies

   B.   Displacement, Extinction, Discouragement, and Diffusion

VI. General Deterrence

   A.   Certainty of Punishment

   B.   Level of Police Activity

   C.   Severity of Punishment

   D.   Capital Punishment

   E.   Swiftness of Punishment

   F.   Critique of General Deterrence

VII. Specific Deterrence

A. RACE, CULTURE, GENDER AND CRIMINOLOGY

   1. Deterring Domestic Violence

VIII. Incapacitation

   A. Can Incapacitation Reduce Crime?

   B. Three Strikes and You're Out

IX. Policy Implications of Choice Theory

CHAPTER REVIEW QUESTIONS

Multiple Choice

1. Using situational crime prevention strategies, which of the following is not a technique designed to increase perceived risks?
   a. entry/exit screening
   b. access control
   c. surveillance by employees
   d. natural surveillance

2. According to Choice Theory, people choose to engage in delinquent and criminal behavior after weighing the _____ of their actions.
   a. costs only
   b. consequences and benefits
   c. benefits only
   d. long-term consequences

3. Rational choice theorists view crime as _____.
   a. offense-specific
   b. offender-specific
   c. both offense- and offender-specific
   d. none of the above

4. According to the rational choice view, crime is a function of a(n) _____ process in which the potential offender weighs the costs and benefits of an illegal act.
   a. decision-making
   b. irrational
   c. psychotic
   d. deterministic

5. Sociologist Jack Katz argues that there are immediate benefits to criminality, which he labels the _____.
   a. seduction of crime
   b. hedonistic approach
   c. get rich quick scheme
   d. winner takes all approach

6. Beccaria developed the _____ school of criminology.
   a. positivist
   b. psychological
   c. sociological
   d. classical

7. Crime prevention tactics used today generally fall in one of four categories including _____.
   a. increase the effort needed to commit crime
   b. increase the risk of committing crime
   c. induce guilt or shame for committing crime
   d. all of the above
   e. none of the above

8. Target reduction strategies are designed to _____.
   a. induce guilt or shame for committing crime
   b. increase the sentences for youthful offenders
   c. reduce the value of crime to the potential criminal
   d. allow police departments to hire more officers

9. The concept of _____ holds that the decision to commit crime can be controlled by the threat of criminal punishment.
   a. specific deterrence
   b. general deterrence
   c. positivism
   d. none of the above

10. According to deterrence theory, crime persists because most criminals believe _____.
    a. there is only a small chance they will get arrested for committing a particular crime
    b. that police officers are sometimes reluctant to make arrests even if they are aware of crime
    c. that even if apprehended there is a good chance of receiving a lenient punishment
    d. all of the above
    e. none of the above

11. In the _____, criminologists focusing on classical ideas of the past, expounded the theme that criminals are rational actors.
    a. 1880s
    b. 1950s
    c. 1960s
    d. 1980s

12. Armed robbers' familiarity with the area gives them ready knowledge of escape routes and is referred to as _____.
    a. crime space
    b. awareness space
    c. rational space
    d. none of the above

13. According to _____ Gary Becker, criminals engage in a cost-benefit analysis of crime.
    a. politician
    b. criminologist
    c. economist
    d. psychologist

14. According to classical criminology, crime can be controlled only by the _____.
    a. police
    b. fear of crime
    c. courts and due process
    d. correct treatment

15. Research shows that robbery levels are relatively _____ in neighborhoods where residents keep a watchful eye on the neighbor's property.
    a. high
    b. low
    c. unstable
    d. unchanged

16. Violent offenders avoid victims who may be _____.
    a. armed and dangerous
    b. nonviolent
    c. under the influence
    d. drug dealers

17. According to rational choice theorists, crime is _____ because criminals evaluate their skills, motives, and needs.
    a. offense-specific
    b. event-specific
    c. offender-specific
    d. all of the above
    e. none of the above

18. Choice theory can be traced to Beccaria's view that crime is rational and can be prevented by punishment that is _____, severe, and certain.
    a. swift
    b. retributive
    c. harsh
    d. none of the above

19. The decision to become a criminal is influenced by _____.
    a. personality
    b. age
    c. status
    d. risk
    e. opportunity
    f. all of the above

20. Research on the direct benefits of incapacitation _____.
    a. has been inconclusive
    b. indicates that incapacitation actually increases the chance of re-offending
    c. indicates that incapacitation is an effective deterrent to criminal behavior
    d. the benefits of incapacitation have not been studied

True/False

1. T / F Rational choice theory has roots in the classical school of criminology.

2. T / F   The concept behind rational choice theory is to let the "punishment fit the crime."

3. T / F   Rational choice theorists view crime as only offender-specific and not offense-specific.

4. T / F   Signs of rationality in the choices of armed robbers are reflected when they generally choose targets near their homes.

5. T / F   According to the rational choice approach, most criminals carefully choose where they will commit their crimes.

6. T / F   Sociologist Jack Katz argues that there are immediate benefits to criminality which he labels the seduction of crime.

7. T / F   Situational crime prevention suggests that crime prevention can be achieved by reducing the opportunities people have to commit particular crimes.

8. T / F   Violent offenders show rationality when they avoid victims who may be armed and dangerous.

9. T / F   Diffusion of benefits occurs when efforts to prevent one crime unintentionally prevent another.

10. T / F   Drug dealers are the most desirable victims of robbers.

11. T / F   If committing crime is a rational choice, it follows that crime can be controlled or eradicated by convincing potential offenders that crime is a poor choice.

12. T / F   A positive relationship should exist between crime rates and the severity, certainty, and speed of legal sanctions.

13. T / F   If the punishment for a crime is increased and the effectiveness and efficiency of the criminal justice system are improved, then the number of people engaging in that crime should increase.

14. T / F   If people believed that their criminal transgressions would result in apprehension and punishment, then only the truly irrational would commit crime.

15. T / F   The certainty of punishment seems to have a greater impact on punishment than severity.

Fill in the Blank

1. _____ helps to structure crime.

2. The excitement or exhilaration of successfully executing illegal activities in dangerous situations is referred to as _____.

3. The three strikes and you're out policy gives people convicted of three felony offenses _____.

4. The concept of criminal choice has prompted the creation of justice policies which treat all offenders equally without regard for their background or personal characteristics. This is referred to as the concept of _____.

5. The just desert model suggests that _____.

6. A method of crime prevention that seeks to eliminate or reduce particular crimes in narrow settings is referred to as _____.

7. Even serial killers use cunning and thought to avoid _____.

8. An effect of crime prevention efforts in which efforts to control crime in one area shift illegal activities to another is referred to as _____.

9. Situational prevention techniques of deflecting offenders include _____.

10. An effect that occurs when limiting access to one target reduces other types of crime as well is referred to as _____.

11. _____ refers to the control of the decision to commit crime by the threat of general punishment.

12. Sudden changes in police activity designed to increase the communicated threat or actual certainty of punishment is known as a _____.

13. The fact that executions may actually increase the likelihood of murders being committed is a consequence referred to as the _____.

14. The view that criminal sanctions should be so powerful that offenders will never repeat their criminal acts is known as _____.

15. The repetition of criminal behavior is referred to as _____.

Essay

1. Rational choice theorists view crime as both offense- and offender-specific. Explain why this is so.

2. Discuss the situational crime prevention approach.

3. Situational crime prevention may produce unforeseen and unwanted consequences. Discuss what is meant by displacement, extinction, discouragement, and diffusion.

4. The theory of specific deterrence holds that criminal sanctions should be so powerful that known criminals will never repeat their criminal acts. Critique this theory. Do you agree with the basic premise of this theory? Why or why not?

5. Discuss whether drug use is rational?

ANSWER KEY FOR CHAPTER REVIEW QUESTIONS

Multiple Choice

1.	(b) access control	p. 82
2.	(b) consequences and benefits	p. 73
3.	(c) both offense- and offender specific	p. 75
4.	(a) decision-making	p. 73
5.	(a) seduction of crime	p. 79
6.	(d) classical	p. 74
7.	(d) all of the above	p. 81
8.	(c) reduce the value of crime to the potential criminal	p. 81
9.	(b) general deterrence	p. 83
10.	(d) all of the above	p. 83
11.	(c) 1960s	p. 74
12.	(b) awareness space	p. 77
13.	(c) economist	p. 74
14.	(b) fear of crime	p. 74
15.	(b) low	p. 77
16.	(a) armed and dangerous	p. 78
17.	(c) offender specific	p. 75
18.	(a) swift	p. 76
19.	(f) all of the above	p. 76
20.	(a) has been inconclusive	p. 88

True/False

1.	True	p. 74
2.	True	p. 74
3.	False	p. 75
4.	True	p. 77
5.	True	p. 75
6.	True	p. 79
7.	True	p. 81
8.	True	p. 78
9.	True	p. 82
10.	True	p. 79
11.	True	p. 79
12.	False	p. 83
13.	False	p. 83
14.	True	p. 83
15.	True	p. 83

Fill in the Blank

1.	place, target, technique	p. 76
2.	edgework	p. 79
3.	a mandatory life term without parole	p. 90
4.	just deserts	p. 92
5.	retribution justifies punishment because people deserve what they get for past deeds	p. 92
6.	situational crime prevention	p. 80
7.	detection	p. 79
8.	displacement	p. 81
9.	bus stop placement, tavern location, street closures	p. 82
10.	discouragement	p. 82
11.	general deterrence	p. 83
12.	crackdown	p. 84
13.	brutalization effect	p. 84
14.	specific deterrence	p. 87
15.	recidivism	p. 87

Essay

1. p. 75
2. pp. 80-2
3. pp. 81-2
4. p. 87
5. p. 78

5 Trait Theory: It's in Their Blood

LEARNING OBJECTIVES

After mastering the content of this chapter, a student should be able to:

1. Understand the concept of sociobiology.
2. Explain what is meant when biosocial theorists use the term equipotentiality.
3. Discuss the relationship between diet and crime.
4. Understand the association between hormones and crime.
5. Discuss why violent offenders may suffer from neurological problems.
6. Explain the factors that make up the ADHD syndrome.
7. Discuss the role genetics plays in violent behavior.
8. Understand the concepts of evolutionary theory.
9. Discuss the psychodynamics of criminality.
10. Understand the association between media and crime.
11. Discuss the role of personality and intelligence in antisocial behaviors.

KEY WORDS AND DEFINITIONS

Trait theory - The view that criminality is a product of abnormal biological or psychological traits.

Sociobiology - The view that human behavior is motivated by inborn biological urges to survive and preserve the species.

Equipotentiality - The view that all humans are born with equal potential to learn and achieve.

Hypoglycemia - A condition that occurs when glucose (sugar) in the blood falls below levels necessary for normal and efficient brain functioning.

Androgens - Male sex hormones.

Testosterone - The principal male hormone.

Premenstrual syndrome (PMS) - The idea that several days prior to and during menstruation, excessive amounts of female sex hormones stimulate antisocial, aggressive behavior.

Neurophysiology - The study of brain activity.

Minimal brain dysfunction (MBD) - An abruptly appearing, maladaptive behavior such as episodic periods of explosive rage.

Attention deficit hyperactivity disorder (ADHD) - A developmentally inappropriate lack of attention, along with impulsivity and hyperactivity.

Neurotransmitters - Chemical compounds that influence or activate brain functions.

Arousal theory - The view that people seek to maintain a preferred level of arousal but vary in how they process sensory input. A need for high levels of environmental stimulation may lead to aggressive, violent behavior patterns.

Monozygotic (MZ) twins - Identical twins.

Dizygotic (DZ) twins - Fraternal (nonidentical) twins.

Cheater theory - A theory suggesting that a subpopulation of men has evolved with genes that incline them toward extremely low parental involvement. Sexually aggressive, they use deceit for sexual conquest of as many females as possible.

Psychodynamic (psychoanalytic) - Theory originated by Freud that the human personality is controlled by unconscious mental processes developed early in childhood, involving the interaction of id, ego, and superego.

Id - The primitive part of people's mental makeup, present at birth, that represents unconscious biological drives for food, sex, and other life-sustaining necessities. The id seeks instant gratification without concern for the rights of others.

Ego - The part of the personality developed in early childhood that helps control the id and keep people's actions within the boundaries of social convention.

Superego - Incorporation within the personality of the moral standards and values of parents, community, and significant others.

Neurotic - In Freudian psychology, a personality marked by mental anguish and feared loss of control.

Psychotic - In Freudian psychology, a personality marked by complete loss of control over the id, characterized by delusions, hallucinations, and sudden mood shifts.

Disorder - Any type of psychological problem (formerly labeled neurotic or psychotic), such as anxiety disorders, mood disorders, and conduct disorders.

Schizophrenia - A severe disorder marked by hearing nonexistent voices, seeing hallucinations, and exhibiting inappropriate responses.

Bipolar disorder - An emotional disturbance in which moods alternate between periods of wild elation and deep depression.

Behavior theory - The view that all human behavior is learned through a process of social reinforcement (rewards and punishment).

Social learning theory - The view that people learn to be aggressive by observing others acting aggressively to achieve some goal or being rewarded for violent acts.

Behavior modeling - Process of learning behavior (notably aggression) by observing others. Aggressive models may be parents, criminals in the neighborhood, or characters on television or in movies.

Cognitive theory - Psychological perspective that focuses on mental processes: how people perceive and mentally represent the world around them and solve problems.

Information-processing theory - Theory that focuses on how people process, store, encode, retrieve, and manipulate information to make decisions and solve problems.

Personality - The reasonably stable patterns of behavior, including thoughts and emotions, that distinguish one person from another.

Antisocial personality - Combination of traits, such as hyperactivity, impulsivity, hedonism, and inability to empathize with others, that make a person prone to deviant behavior and violence; also referred to as sociopathic or psychopathic personality.

Nature theory - The view that intelligence is largely determined genetically and that low intelligence is linked to criminal behavior.

Nurture theory - The view that intelligence is not inherited but is largely a product of environment. Low IQ scores do not cause crime but may result from the same environmental factors.

Primary prevention programs - Programs, such as substance abuse clinics and mental health associations, that seek to treat personal problems before they manifest themselves as crime.

Secondary prevention programs - Programs that provide treatment such as psychological counseling to youths and adults after they have violated the law.

CHAPTER SUMMARY

The earliest positivist criminologists were biologists. Led by Cesare Lombroso, these early researchers believed that some people manifested primitive traits that made them born criminals. Today their research is debunked because of poor methodology, testing, and logic. Biological views fell out of favor in the early twentieth century. In the 1970s, spurred by the publication of Edmund O. Wilson's Sociobiology, several criminologists again turned to study of the biological basis of criminality. For the most part, the effort has focused on the cause of violent crime.

One area of interest is biochemical factors, such as diet, allergies, hormonal imbalances, and environmental contaminants (such as lead). The conclusion is that crime, especially violence, is a function of diet, vitamin intake, hormonal imbalance, or food allergies. Neurophysiological factors, such as brain disorders, ADHD, EEG abnormalities, tumors, and head injuries have been linked to crime. Criminals and delinquents often suffer brain impairment, as measured by the EEG.

Attention deficit hyperactivity disorder and minimal brain dysfunction are related to antisocial behavior. Some biocriminologists believe that the tendency to commit violent acts is inherited. Research has been conducted with twin pairs and adopted children to determine whether genes are related to behaviors. An evolutionary branch holds that changes in the human condition, which have taken millions of years to evolve, may help explain crime rate differences. As the human race evolved, traits and characteristics have become ingrained.

The psychodynamic view, developed by Sigmund Freud, links aggressive behavior to personality conflicts arising from childhood. The development of the unconscious personality early in childhood influences behavior for the rest of a person's life. Criminals have weak egos and damaged personalities. According to some psychoanalysts, psychotics are aggressive, unstable people who can easily become involved in crime.

Cognitive psychology is concerned with human development and how people perceive the world. Criminality is viewed as a function of improper information processing. Individual reasoning processes influence behavior. Reasoning is influenced by the way people perceive their environment.

Behavioral and social learning theorists see criminality as a learned behavior. Children who are exposed to violence and see it rewarded may become violent as adults. People commit crime when they model their behavior after others they see being rewarded for the same acts. Behavior is reinforced by rewards and extinguished by punishment. Psychological traits such as personality and intelligence have been linked to criminality.

One important area of study has been the antisocial personality, a person who lacks emotion and concern for others. The controversial issue of the relationship of IQ to criminality has been resurrected once again with the publication of research studies purporting to show that criminals have lower IQs than noncriminals.

CHAPTER OUTLINE

I.   The Development of Trait Theory
II. Contemporary Trait Theory
III. Biological Trait Theories
    A. Biochemical Conditions and Crime
    B. CURRENT ISSUES IN CRIME
        1. Are You What You Eat?
    C. Neurophysiological Conditions and Crime
    D. Genetics and Crime
    E. Evolutionary Views of Crime
    F. Evaluation of the Biological Branch of Trait Theory
IV. Psychological Trait Theories
    A. Psychodynamic Perspective
    B. Behavioral Perspective:
    C. Social Learning Theory
    D. Cognitive Theory
    E. Personality and Crime
    F. Intelligence and Crime
V.   Social Policy Implications

CHAPTER REVIEW QUESTIONS

Multiple Choice

1. _____ occurs when blood glucose (sugar) falls below levels necessary for normal and efficient brain functioning.
    a. Hypothermia
    b. Hypoglycemia
    c. Hyporeactivity
    d. Hyposugaracetate

2. Symptoms of hypoglycemia include all of the following except _____.
   a. anxiety
   b. sleepiness
   c. depression
   d. confusion

3. Hormones are linked to emotional volatility and influence _____ of the neocortex.
   a. the left hemisphere
   b. the right hemisphere
   c. both hemispheres
   d. neither hemispheres

4. Besides aggressive behavior, other androgen-related male traits include _____.
   a. sensation seeking
   b. impulsivity
   c. dominance
   d. reduced verbal skills
   e. all of the above
   f. none of the above

5. Research conducted on both human and animal subjects has found that _____ exposure to unnaturally high levels of testosterone permanently alters behavior.
   a. prenatal
   b. postnatal
   c. postneonatal
   d. all of the above
   e. none of the above

6. The study of brain activity is referred to as _____.
   a. neuropsychology
   b. neurosociology
   c. neurocriminology
   d. neurophysiology

7. Studies measuring the presence of minimal brain dysfunction in offender populations have found that up to _____ percent exhibit brain dysfunction on psychological tests.
   a. 30
   b. 40
   c. 50
   d. 60

8. A developmentally inappropriate lack of attention, along with impulsivity and hyperactivity is known as _____.
   a. attention deficit personality disorder
   b. attention deficit criminality disorder
   c. attention deficit hyperactivity disorder
   d. attention deficit medical disorder

9. Murderers exhibit brain pathology at a rate _____ times greater than that in the general population.
   a. 22
   b. 32
   c. 42
   d. 52

10. Chemical compounds that influence or activate brain functions are known as _____.
    a. neurotransformers
    b. neurofunctioners
    c. neurobrain power
    d. neurotransmitters

11. Studies of habitually violent criminals show that _____ serotonin levels are associated with poor impulse control and hyperactivity.
    a. high
    b. low
    c. very high
    d. stable

12. According to Freud, the primitive part of people's makeup which seeks instant gratification is referred to as the _____.
    a. Id
    b. Ego
    c. Superego
    d. Psychodynamic

13. According to Freud, the part of the personality developed in early childhood that keeps people's actions within the boundaries of social convention is referred to as the _____.
    a. Id
    b. Ego
    c. Superego
    d. Psychodynamic

14. According to Freud, the _____ is the incorporation within the personality of the moral standards and values of parents, community, and significant others.
    a. Id
    b. Ego
    c. Superego
    d. Psychodynamic

15. The term "psychotic" has been replaced today with the term _____.
    a. neurotic
    b. schizophrenic
    c. psychodynamic
    d. disorder

16. The most serious psychodynamic disorder is _____.
    a. sociopathology
    b. psychopathy
    c. antisocial personality
    d. schizophrenia

17. Psychodynamic theorists view criminals as _____ -dominated persons who suffer from one or more disorders.
    a. Id
    b. Ego
    c. Superego
    d. Psychodynamic

18. An emotional disturbance in which moods alternate between periods of wild elation and deep depression is known as _____.
    a. narcissistic disorder
    b. bipolar disorder
    c. histrionic disorder
    d. antisocial disorder

19. Social learning theorists view violence as something learned through a process called _____ modeling.
    a. parental
    b. peer
    c. behavior
    d. family

20. Social learning theorists suggest that all of the following factors except _____ may contribute to violent or aggressive behavior.
    a. a heightened arousal event
    b. unexpected outcomes
    c. aggressive skills
    d. expected outcomes
    e. consistency of behavior with values

True/False

1. T / F Biological explanations of crime fell out of favor and were abandoned in the early 18th century.

2. T / F Biosocial research has found that abnormal levels of male sex hormones, known as estrogens, do in fact produce aggressive behavior.

3. T / F The link between PMS and crime is tenuous at best.

4. T / F Criminologists who focus on the biological conditions that control human behavior refer to themselves as contemporary trait criminologists.

5. T / F MBD stands for minimal brain dysfunction.

6. T / F About 20 percent of U.S. children, most often boys, are believed to suffer from ADHD.

7. T / F Brain structure, brain damage, and brain chemicals are the causes of behavior in the neurophysiological perspective.

8. T / F Research shows that women in common-law marriages, especially those who are much younger than their husbands, are at greater risk of abuse than older, married women.

9. T / F The most significant criticism of biosocial theory has been that it is outdated.

10. T / F Genetic theory holds that violence-producing traits are found only in males.

11. T / F According to Freud, the Id develops as a result of incorporating within the personality the moral standards and values of parents, community, and significant others.

12. T / F Cognitive theory is the branch of behavior theory most relevant to criminology.

13. T / F In 1977 Travis Hirschi and Michael Hindelang published a widely read article linking intelligence and crime.

14. T / F The "Twinkie defense" promoted the view that biochemical conditions influence antisocial behavior.

15. T / F According to biosocial theorists, females are biologically and naturally more aggressive than males.

Fill in the Blank

1. The two major categories of trait theory are _____ and _____.

2. Biological explanations of crime once again reemerged in the early _____.

3. _____, the most abundant androgen, has been linked to criminality.

4. Criminologist Deborah Denno investigated the behavior of more than 900 African-American youths and found that _____ was one of the most significant predictors of male delinquency and persistent adult criminality.

5. Diet, hormones, and contaminants are the causes of behavior in the _____ perspective.

6. Episodic periods of explosive rage have been found to be related to _____.

7. Cohort data gathered by Donald West and David Farrington indicate that a significant number of delinquent youths have _____.

8. According to _____ theory, a subpopulation of men has evolved with genes that incline them toward extremely low parental involvement.

9. _____ was the forerunner of modern learning theorists who believed that people learn from one another through imitation.

10. Aggression evolving over time and aggressive males producing more offspring are causes of behavior according to the _____ perspective.

11. Biosocial research has found that abnormal levels of androgens produce _____ behavior.

12. According to cheater theory, a subpopulation of _____ has evolved with genes that incline them toward extremely low parental involvement.

13. Because twins reared apart are so similar, the _____, if anything, makes them different.

14. Brain chemistry and hormonal differences are related to aggression and _____.

15. The id seeks _____ without concern for the rights of others.

Essay

1. Trait theories have gained prominence recently. Discuss why this is the case.

2. Discuss how the relationship between genetics and crime has been studied and what is known from this research.

3. Evaluate the biological branch of trait theory.

4. Discuss whether the mentally ill population has a greater inclination toward criminal behavior than the mentally sound.

5. Discuss the three principal sources upon which aggressive acts are usually modeled according to social learning theorists.

ANSWER KEY FOR CHAPTER REVIEW QUESTIONS

Multiple Choice

1.	(b) hypoglycemia	p. 100
2.	(b) sleepiness	p. 100
3.	(a) the left hemisphere	p. 100
4.	(e) all of the above	pp. 100-101
5.	(a) prenatal	p. 102
6.	(d) neurophysiology	p. 103
7.	(d) 60	p. 103
8.	(c) Attention Deficit Hyperactivity Disorder	p. 103
9.	(b) 32	p. 103
10.	(d) Neurotransmitters	p. 104
11.	(b) low	p. 105
12.	(a) Id	p. 111
13.	(b) Ego	p. 112
14.	(c) Superego	p. 112
15.	(d) disorder	p. 112
16.	(d) schizophrenia	p. 112
17.	(a) Id	p. 113
18.	(b) bipolar disorder	p. 113
19.	(c) behavior	p. 114
20.	(b) unexpected outcomes	pp.115-16

True/False

1.	False	p. 98
2.	False	p. 100
3.	True	p. 102
4.	False	p. 99
5.	True	p. 103
6.	False	p. 104
7.	True	p. 99
8.	True	p. 109
9.	False	p. 110
10.	False	p. 111
11.	False	p. 112
12.	False	p. 114
13.	True	p. 119
14.	True	pp. 99-100
15.	False	p. 100

Fill in the Blank

1. biological and psychological   p. 98
2. 1970s   p. 98
3. Testosterone   p. 102
4. lead poisoning   p. 102
5. biochemical   p. 99
6. MBD   p. 103
7. criminal fathers   p. 106
8. cheater theory   pp. 109-110
9. Gabriel Tarde   p. 111
10. evolutionary   p. 99
11. aggressive   p. 100
12. men   p. 109
13. environmental   p. 108
14. violence   p. 110
15. instant gratification   p. 111

Essay

1. p. 99
2. pp. 106-9
3. p. 110
4. p. 114
5. pp. 114-5

6 Social Structure Theory: Because They're Poor

LEARNING OBJECTIVES

After mastering the content of this chapter, a student should be able to:

1. Understand the concept of social structure.
2. Explain the socioeconomic structure of American society.
3. Discuss the concept of social disorganization.
4. Explain the works of Shaw and McKay.
5. Describe what is meant by concentric zone theory.
6. Discuss the various elements of ecological theory.
7. Discuss the association between collective efficacy and crime.
8. Understand the concept of strain.
9. Explain what is meant by the term anomie.
10. Understand the concept of cultural deviance.

KEY WORDS AND DEFINITIONS

Stratified society - People grouped according to economic or social class; characterized by the unequal distribution of wealth, power, and prestige.

Social class - Segment of the population whose members are at a relatively similar economic level and who share attitudes, values, norms, and an identifiable lifestyle.

Truly disadvantaged - The lowest level of the underclass; urban, inner-city, socially isolated people who occupy the bottom rung of the social ladder and are the victims of discrimination.

Culture of poverty - A separate lower-class culture, characterized by apathy, cynicism, helplessness, and mistrust of social institutions such as schools, government agencies, and the police that is passed from one generation to the next.

Underclass - The lowest social stratum in any country, whose members lack the education and skills needed to function successfully in modern society.

Social structure theory - The view that disadvantaged economic class position is a primary cause of crime.

Social disorganization theory - Branch of social structure theory that focuses on the breakdown of institutions such as the family, school, and employment in inner-city neighborhoods.

Strain theory - Branch of social structure theory that sees crime as a function of the conflict between people's goals and the means available to obtain them.

Strain - The anger, frustration, and resentment experienced by people who believe they cannot achieve their goals through legitimate means.

Cultural deviance theory - Branch of social structure theory that sees strain and social disorganization together resulting in a unique lower-class culture that conflicts with conventional social norms.

Subculture - A set of values, beliefs, and traditions unique to a particular social class or group within a larger society.

Cultural transmission - Process whereby values, beliefs, and traditions are handed down from one generation to the next.

Transitional neighborhood - An area undergoing a shift in population and structure, usually from middle-class residential to lower-class mixed use.

Concentration effect - As working- and middle-class families flee inner-city poverty areas, the most disadvantaged population is consolidated in urban ghettos.

Collective efficacy - Social control exerted by cohesive communities, based on mutual trust, including intervention in the supervision of children and maintenance of public order.

Social altruism - Voluntary mutual support systems, such as neighborhood associations and self-help groups, that reinforce moral and social obligations.

Anomie - A lack of norms or clear social standards. Because of rapidly shifting moral values, the individual has few guides to what is socially acceptable.

Anomie theory - View that anomie results when socially defined goals (such as wealth and power) are universally mandated but access to legitimate means (such as education and job opportunities) is stratified by class and status.

Institutional anomie theory - The view that anomie pervades U.S. culture because the drive for material wealth dominates and undermines social and community values.

American Dream - The goal of accumulating material goods and wealth through individual competition; the process of being socialized to pursue material success and to believe it is achievable.

Relative deprivation - Envy, mistrust, and aggression resulting from perceptions of economic and social inequality.

General strain theory (GST) - The view that multiple sources of strain interact with an individual's emotional traits and responses to produce criminality.

Negative affective states - Anger, frustration, and adverse emotions produced by a variety of sources of strain.

Focal concerns - Values, such as toughness and street smarts, that have evolved specifically to fit conditions in lower-class environments.

Delinquent subculture - A value system adopted by lower-class youths that is directly opposed to that of the larger society.

Status frustration - A form of culture conflict experienced by lower-class youths because social conditions prevent them from achieving success as defined by the larger society.

Middle-class measuring rods - The standards by which authority figures, such as teachers and employers, evaluate lower-class youngsters and often prejudge them negatively.

Reaction formation - Irrational hostility evidenced by young delinquents, who adopt norms directly opposed to middle-class goals and standards that seem impossible to achieve.

Differential opportunity - The view that lower-class youths, whose legitimate opportunities are limited, join gangs and pursue criminal careers as alternative means to achieve universal success goals.

CHAPTER SUMMARY

Sociology has been the main orientation of criminologists because they know that crime rates vary among elements of the social structure, that society goes through changes that affect crime, and that social interaction relates to criminality. Social structure theories suggest that people's place in the socioeconomic structure influences their chances of becoming criminals. Poor people are more likely to commit crimes because they are unable to achieve monetary or social success in any other way. Social structure theory includes three schools of thought: social disorganization, strain, and cultural deviance theories.

Social disorganization theory suggests that the urban poor violate the law because they live in areas in which social control has broken down. The origin of social disorganization theory can be traced to the work of Clifford R. Shaw and Henry D. McKay. Shaw and McKay concluded that disorganized areas, marked by divergent values and transitional populations, produce criminality. Modern social ecology theory looks at such issues as community fear, unemployment, and deterioration. Strain theories view crime as resulting from the anger people experience over their inability to achieve legitimate social and economic success.

Strain theories hold that most people share common values and beliefs, but the ability to achieve them is differentiated by the social structure. The best-known strain theory is Robert Merton's theory of anomie, which describes what happens when people have inadequate means to satisfy their goals. Steven Messner and Richard Rosenfeld show that the core values of American culture produces strain. Robert Agnew suggests that strain has multiple sources and is linked to anger and frustration that people endure when their goals and aspirations are frustrated or when they lose something they value.

Cultural deviance theories hold that a unique value system develops in lower-class areas. Lower-class values approve of behaviors such as being tough, never showing fear, and defying authority. People perceiving strain will bond together in their own groups or subcultures for support and recognition. Albert Cohen links the formation of subcultures to the failure of lower-class citizens to achieve recognition from middle-class decision makers, such as teachers, employers, and police officers. Richard Cloward and Lloyd Ohlin have argued that crime results from lower-class people's perception that their opportunity for success is limited. Consequently, youths in low-income areas may join criminal, conflict, or retreatist gangs.

CHAPTER OUTLINE

I. Economic Structure and Crime
    A. Child Poverty
    B. Lower-Class Culture
    C. Minority Group Poverty
    D. RACE, CULTURE, GENDER AND CRIMINOLOGY
        1. Bridging the Racial Divide

CHAPTER REVIEW QUESTIONS

Multiple Choice

1. Segment of the population whose members are at a relatively similar economic level and who share attitudes, values, norms, and an identifiable lifestyle.
   a. stratified society
   b. social class
   c. lower class
   d. upper class

2. The lowest level of the underclass is also referred to as the _____.
   a. lower class
   b. lower lower class
   c. truly disadvantaged
   d. ultimate lower class

3. The lowest social stratum in any country, whose members lack the education and skills needed to function successfully in modern society, is referred to as the _____.
   a. culture of poverty
   b. lower class
   c. truly disadvantaged
   d. underclass

4. Social disorganization theory is the branch of social structure theory that focuses on the breakdown of institutions such as the _____ in inner city neighborhoods.
   a. family
   b. school
   c. job market
   d. all of the above
   e. none of the above

5. According to strain theory, people feel _____ because they are unable to achieve success through conventional means.
   a. anger
   b. frustration
   c. resentment
   d. all of the above
   e. none of the above

6. The branches of social structure theory include _____.
   a. social disorganization theory
   b. cultural deviance theory
   c. strain theory
   d. all of the above
   e. none of the above

7. Community deterioration includes all of the following except _____.
   a. disorder
   b. poverty
   c. alienation
   d. high real estate rates
   e. disassociation
   f. fear of crime

8. The forms of collective efficacy include all of the following except _____.
   a. informal social control
   b. personal social control
   c. institutional social control
   d. public social control

9. Sources of institutional social control include all of the following except _____.
   a. families
   b. businesses
   c. stores
   d. schools
   e. churches

10. One of the primary sources of public social control is _____.
    a. schools
    b. policing
    c. families
    d. peers

11. According to strain theory, the ability to achieve personal goals is stratified by _____.
    a. age
    b. gender
    c. socioeconomic class
    d. none of the above

12. Merton argues that in the United States legitimate means to acquire wealth are stratified across _____ lines.
    a. class
    b. gender
    c. status
    d. age
    e. a and b only
    f. a and c only

13. Merton's social adaptation that occurs when individuals embrace conventional goals and also have the means to attain them is referred to as _____.
    a. conformity
    b. innovation
    c. ritualism
    d. retreatism
    e. rebellion

14. Merton's social adaptation that involves substituting an alternative set of goals and means for conventional ones is referred to as _____.
    a. conformity
    b. innovation
    c. ritualism
    d. retreatism
    e. rebellion

15. Merton's social adaptation that occurs when individuals accept the goals of society but are unable to attain them through legitimate means so they innovate is referred to as _____.
    a. conformity
    b. innovation
    c. ritualism
    d. retreatism
    e. rebellion

16. According to Merton, _____ occurs when people reject both the goals and the means of society and escape their lack of success.
    a. conformity
    b. innovation
    c. ritualism
    d. retreatism
    e. rebellion

17. According to Merton, _____ occurs when people gain pleasure from practicing traditional ceremonies, regardless of whether they have a real purpose or goal.
    a. conformity
    b. innovation
    c. ritualism
    d. retreatism
    e. rebellion

18. According to Messner and Rosenfeld, the relatively high crime rates can be explained by the interrelationship of _____.
    a. culture and anomie
    b. anomie and institutions
    c. culture and institutions
    d. none of the above

19. Sociologist Robert Agnew's general strain theory (GST) helps identify the _____ - level influences of strain.
    a. micro
    b. individual
    c. macro
    d. institutional
    e. societal
    f. b and c only
    g. a and b only

20. Agnew (GST) suggests that criminality is the direct result of the anger, frustration, and adverse emotions that emerge in the wake of destructive social relationships. He refers to these emotions as _____.
    a. relative deprivation
    b. general strain
    c. negative affective states
    d. all of the above
    e. none of the above

True/False

1. T / F Some criminologists believe that destructive social forces in poverty areas are responsible for high crime rates.

2. T / F Subcultural values are handed down from one generation to the next in a process called value transmission.

3. T / F Social disorganization theory was popularized by the work of Lombroso and Goring.

4. T / F According to Shaw and McKay, the zones farthest from the city's center had correspondingly lower crime rates.

5. T / F As working- and middle-class families flee inner-city poverty areas, the most disadvantaged population is consolidated in urban ghettos. This effect is known as the consolidation effect.

6. T / F All three forms of collective efficacy contribute to community stability.

7. T / F The level of policing from neighborhood to neighborhood is typically consistent.

8. T / F Shaw and McKay found stable patterns of crime in the central city.

9. T / F Ecological theorists view crime as a direct result of lower class frustration and anger.

10. T / F Agnew (GST) offers a more general explanation of criminal activity among all elements of society rather than restricting his views to lower-class crime.

11. T / F Agnew's general theory of strain suggests that there is only one source of anomie.

12. T / F Miller's lower class focus concerns include trouble, toughness, and fate.

13. T / F According to Miller, clinging to lower-class focal concerns promotes illegal or violent behavior.

14. T / F The centerpiece of Cloward and Ohlin's theory is the concept of relative deprivation.

15. T / F The best known strain theory is Robert Merton's theory of anomie, which describes what happens when people have adequate means to satisfy their goals.

Fill in the Blank

1. People in the United States live in a _____ society.

2. In 1970, Gunnar Myrdal described a worldwide _____ that was cut off from society, its members lacking the education and skills needed to function successfully in modern society.

3. Strain theory sees crime as a function of the _____ between people's _____ and the _____ available to obtain them.

4. Because crime rates are higher in lower-class areas, many criminologists believe that the causes of crime are rooted in _____ factors.

5. A set of values, beliefs, and traditions unique to a particular social class or group within a larger society is known as _____.

6. In larger cities, abandoned buildings serve as a "_____."

7. Communities characterized by mutual trust, a willingness to intervene in the supervision of children and the maintenance of public order have developed _____.

8. _____ is the voluntary mutual support systems, such as neighborhood associations and self-help groups that reinforce moral and social obligations.

9. A lack of norms or clear social standards is referred to as _____.

10. The process of being socialized to pursue material success and to believe it is achievable is known as the _____.

11. Envy, mistrust, and aggression resulting from perceptions of economic and social inequality are referred to as _____.

12. According to Miller, the values, such as toughness and street smarts, that have evolved specifically to fit conditions in lower-class environments is referred to as _____.

13. A value system adopted by lower-class youths that is directly opposed to that of the larger society is referred to as _____.

14. The standards by which authority figures, such as teachers and employers, evaluate lower-class youngsters and often prejudge them negatively is referred to as

_____.

15. Because of differential opportunity, young people are likely to join one of three types of gangs which include _____, _____, and

_____.

Essay

1. Discuss the association between family poverty and children's health, achievement, and behavior impairments.

2. Discuss the relationship between a siege mentality and allegations of excessive force against the police.

3. Discuss the three forms of collective efficacy and how they contribute to community stability.

4. How does strain affect criminal activities?

5. Discuss Merton's social adaptations and how they relate to criminal behavior.

ANSWER KEY FOR CHAPTER REVIEW QUESTIONS

Multiple Choice

1.	(b) social class	p. 126
2.	(c) truly disadvantaged	p. 128
3.	(d) underclass	p. 129
4.	(d) all of the above	p. 130
5.	(d) all of the above	p. 131
6.	(d) all of the above	p. 131
7.	(d) high real estate rates	p. 134
8.	(b) personal social control	p. 137
9.	(a) families	p. 137
10.	(b) policing	p. 137
11.	(c) socioeconomic class	p. 139
12.	(f) a and c only	p. 139
13.	(a) conformity	pp. 139-40
14.	(e) rebellion	pp. 139-40
15.	(b) innovation	pp. 139-40
16.	(d) retreatism	pp. 139-40
17.	(c) ritualism	pp. 139-40
18.	(c) culture and institutions	p. 142
19.	(g) a and b only	p. 143
20.	(c) negative affective states	p. 143

True/False

1.	True	p. 131
2.	False	p. 131
3.	False	p. 132
4.	True	p. 133
5.	False	p. 136
6.	True	p. 137
7.	False	p. 137
8.	True	p. 138
9.	False	p. 139
10.	True	p. 143
11.	False	p. 145
12.	True	p. 147
13.	True	p. 147
14.	False	p. 148
15.	False	p. 151

Fill in the Blank

1.	stratified	p. 126
2.	underclass	p. 129
3.	conflict, goals, means	p. 130
4.	socioeconomic	p. 131
5.	subculture	p. 132
6.	magnet for crime	p. 134
7.	collective efficacy	p. 136
8.	social altruism	p. 138
9.	anomie	p. 139
10.	American Dream	p. 141
11.	relative deprivation	p. 142
12.	focal concerns	p. 146
13.	delinquent subculture	p. 147
14.	middle-class measuring rod	p. 148
15.	criminal, conflict, retreatist	p. 149

Essay

1. pp. 127-9
2. pp. 135-6
3. pp. 137-8
4. pp. 139-41
5. pp. 139-40

7 Social Process Theories: Socialized to Crime

LEARNING OBJECTIVES

After mastering the content of this chapter, a student should be able to:

1. Explain the concept of socialization.
2. Discuss the effect of schools, family, and friends on crime.
3. Discuss the differences between learning, control, and reaction.
4. Understand the concept of differential association.
5. Discuss what is meant by a definition toward criminality.
6. Understand the concept of neutralization.
7. Discuss the relationship between self-concept and crime.
8. Explain the elements of the social bond.
9. Describe the labeling process.
10. Understand the concepts of primary and secondary deviance.
11. Explain how the process of labeling leads to criminal careers.

KEY WORDS AND DEFINITIONS

Socialization - Process of human development and enculturation. Socialization is influenced by key social processes and institutions.

Social process theory - The view that criminality is a function of people's interactions with various organizations, institutions, and processes in society.

Parental efficacy - Parents who are supportive and effectively control their children in a noncoercive fashion.

Social learning theory - The view that people learn to be aggressive by observing others acting aggressively to achieve some goal or being rewarded for violent acts.

Social control theory - The view that people commit crime when the forces binding them to society are weakened or broken.

Social reaction (labeling) theory - The view that people become criminals when labeled as such and when they accept the label as a personal identity.

Differential association theory - The view that people commit crime when their social learning leads them to perceive more definitions favoring crime than favoring conventional behavior.

Culture conflict - Result of exposure to opposing norms, attitudes, and definitions of right and wrong, moral and immoral.

Neutralization theory - The view that law violators learn to neutralize conventional values and attitudes, enabling them to drift back and forth between criminal and conventional behavior.

Drift - Movement in and out of delinquency, shifting between conventional and deviant values.

Neutralization techniques - Methods of rationalizing deviant behavior, such as denying responsibility or blaming the victim.

Self-control - A strong moral sense that renders a person incapable of hurting others or violating social norms.

Commitment to conformity - A strong personal investment in conventional institutions, individuals, and processes that prevents people from engaging in behavior that might jeopardize their reputation and achievements.

Social bonds - The ties that bind people to society, including relationships with friends, family, neighbors, teachers, and employers. Elements of the social bond include commitment, attachment, involvement, and belief.

Stigmatize - To apply negative labeling with enduring effects on a person's self-image and social interactions.

Moral entrepreneur - A person who creates moral rules that reflect the values of those in power rather than any objective, universal standards of right and wrong.

Successful degradation ceremony - A course of action or ritual in which someone's identity is publicly redefined and destroyed and they are thereafter viewed as socially unacceptable.

Retrospective reading - The reassessment of a person's past to fit a current generalized label.

Primary deviance - A norm violation or crime with little or no long-term influence on the violator.

Secondary deviance - A norm violation or crime that comes to the attention of significant others or social control agents, who apply a negative label with long-term consequences for the violator's self-identity and social interactions.

Deviance amplification - Process whereby secondary deviance pushes offenders out of mainstream of society and locks them into an escalating cycle of deviance, apprehension, labeling, and criminal self-identity.

Reflected appraisal - When parents are alienated from their children, their negative labeling reduces their children's self-image and increases delinquency.

Diversion programs - Programs of rehabilitation that remove offenders from the normal channels of the criminal justice process, thus avoiding the stigma of a criminal label.

Restitution - Permitting an offender to repay the victim or do useful work in the community rather than face the stigma of a formal trial and a court-ordered sentence.

CHAPTER SUMMARY

Social process theories view criminality as a function of people's interaction with various organizations, institutions, and processes in society. People in all walks of life have the potential to become criminals if they maintain destructive social relationships. Improper socialization is a key component of crime. Social process theory has three main branches. Social learning theory stresses that people learn how to commit crimes. Social control theory analyzes the failure of society to control criminal tendencies. Labeling theory maintains that negative labels produce criminal careers.

Social learning theory suggests that people learn criminal behaviors much as they learn conventional behavior. Differential association theory, formulated by Edwin Sutherland, holds that criminality is a result of a person's perceiving an excess of definitions in favor of crime over definitions that uphold conventional values. Sykes and Matza's theory of neutralization stresses that youths learn behavior rationalizations that enable them to overcome societal values and norms and break the law.

Control theory maintains that all people have the potential to become criminals, but their bonds to conventional society prevent them from violating the law. This view suggests that a person's self-concept aids his or her commitment to conventional action. Travis Hirschi's social control theory describes the social bond as containing elements of attachment, commitment, involvement, and belief. Weakened bonds allow youths to behave antisocially.

Social reaction or labeling theory holds that criminality is promoted by becoming negatively labeled by significant others. Such labels as "criminal," "ex-con," and "junkie" isolate people from society and lock them into lives of crime. Labels create expectations that the labeled person will act in a certain way; labeled people are always watched and suspected. Eventually these people begin to accept their labels as personal identities, locking them further into lives of crime and deviance. Edwin Lemert suggests that people who accept labels are involved in secondary deviance while primary deviants are able to maintain an undamaged identity. Unfortunately, research on labeling has not supported its major premises. Consequently, critics have charged that it lacks credibility as a description of crime causation. Social process theories have greatly influenced social policy. They have controlled treatment orientations as well as community action policies.

CHAPTER OUTLINE

I.   Socialization and Crime
- A. Family Relations
- B. Educational Experience
- C. Peer Relations
- D. Religious Belief
- E. The Effects of Socialization on Crime

II. Social Learning Theories
- A. Differential Association Theory
- B. Neutralization Theory
- C. Are Learning Theories Valid?

III. Social Control Theory
- A. Self-Concept and Crime
- B. Contemporary Social Control Theory
- C. Testing Social Control Theory

IV. Social Reaction (Labeling) Theory
- A. Consequences of Labeling
- B. Primary and Secondary Deviance

C. Crime and Labeling Theory

D. Differential Enforcement

E. Research on Social Reaction Theory

F. Is Labeling Theory Valid?

V. Social Process Theory and Public Policy

   A. POLICY AND PRACTICE IN CRIMINOLOGY

      1. Head Start

CHAPTER REVIEW QUESTIONS

Multiple Choice

1. Parents who are supportive and effectively control their children in a noncoercive fashion are more likely to raise children who refrain from delinquency. This is referred to as _____.
   a. socialization
   b. social efficacy
   c. parental efficacy
   d. social process

2. The theory that criminality is a function of people's interactions with various organizations, institutions, and processes in society is known as _____ theory.
   a. social learning
   b. social process
   c. social control
   d. social reaction

3. Children who _____ are the most likely to engage in criminal acts.
   a. do poorly in school
   b. lack educational motivation
   c. feel alienated
   d. all of the above
   e. none of the above

4. Schools label students when they use the _____ system which identifies some students as college-bound and others as academic underachievers or potential dropouts.
   a. IQ
   b. reading
   c. track
   d. intelligence
   e. none of the above

5. _____ theory suggests that people learn the techniques and attitudes of crime from close relationships with criminal peers.
   a. Social learning
   b. Social process
   c. Social control
   d. Social reaction

6. _____ theory suggests that people commit crime when the forces binding them to society are weakened or broken.
   a. Social learning
   b. Social process
   c. Social control
   d. Social reaction

7. _____ theory suggests that people become criminals when labeled as such and when they accept the label as a personal identity.
   a. Social learning
   b. Social process
   c. Social control
   d. Social reaction

8. The most prominent form(s) of social learning theory is (are) _____.
   a. differential neutralization theory
   b. differential association theory
   c. neutralization theory
   d. a and b only
   e. a and c only

9. According to Sutherland, acquiring a behavior is a socialization process, not a _____ process.
   a. psychological
   b. political
   c. legal
   d. a and c only
   e. b and c only

10. According to Sutherland, skills and motives conducive to crime are learned as a result of contact with _____.
    a. pro-crime values
    b. attitudes
    c. definitions
    d. other patterns of criminal behavior
    e. all of the above
    f. none of the above

11. The conflict of social attitudes and cultural norms is the basis for the concept of _____.
    a. differential neutralization
    b. labeling
    c. differential association
    d. self control
    e. none of the above

12. Differential association may vary in _____.
    a. frequency
    b. duration
    c. priority
    d. intensity
    e. all of the above
    f. none of the above

13. According to differential association theory, the following are ideas that prohibit crime except _____.
    a. play fair
    b. the end justifies the mean
    c. don't be a bully
    d. forgive and forget
    e. honesty is the best policy

14. According to differential association theory, the following are ideas that justify crime except _____.
    a. drinking is ok
    b. don't let anyone push you around
    c. I don't get even, I get mad
    d. turn the other cheek

15. Movement in and out of delinquency, shifting between conventional and deviant values is known as _____.
    a. shift
    b. drift
    c. slide
    d. slip

16. According to Sykes and Matza, the technique of neutralization that is used when young offenders sometimes claim that their unlawful acts are not their fault but from forces beyond their control or accident is referred to as _____.
    a. denial of responsibility
    b. denial of injury
    c. denial of victim
    d. condemnation of the condemners
    e. appeal to higher loyalties

17. According to Sykes and Matza, the technique of neutralization that is used when offenders claim that the victim "had it coming" is referred to as _____.
    a. denial of responsibility
    b. denial of injury
    c. denial of victim
    d. condemnation of the condemners
    e. appeal to higher loyalties

18. According to Sykes and Matza, the technique of neutralization that is used when offenders view the world as a corrupt place and they are no worse than those in authority such as police and judges who are corrupt is referred to as _____.
    a. denial of responsibility
    b. denial of injury
    c. denial of victim
    d. condemnation of the condemners
    e. appeal to higher loyalties

19. Learning theories help explain the important role that _____ play in shaping criminal and conventional behaviors.
    a. peers
    b. family
    c. education
    d. all of the above
    e. none of the above

20. Early versions of control theory speculated that criminality was a product of _____.
    a. strong self-concept
    b. weak self-concept
    c. poor self-esteem
    d. good self-esteem
    e. a and d only
    f. b and c only

True/False

1. T / F Family relationships are not considered a major determinant of behavior.

2. T / F High self-esteem is inversely related to criminal behavior.

3. T / F Adolescents who do not receive affection from their parents during childhood are not more likely to use illicit drugs and be more aggressive as they mature.

4. T / F Children growing up in homes where a parent suffers mental impairment are also at risk for delinquency.

5. T / F Children whose parents abuse drugs are not more likely to become persistent substance abusers than the children of non-abusers.

6. T / F Children who experience abuse, neglect, or sexual abuse are believed to be more crime prone.

7. T / F Children who fail in school are no more likely to offend than those who do not fail in school.

8. T / F Actually attending religious services has a more dramatic effect on behavior than merely holding religious beliefs.

9. T / F Educational failure has not been linked to criminality.

10. T / F Social learning assumes that people are born bad and must be controlled in order to be good.

11. T / F Contacts made early in life probably have more influence than those developed later on.

12. T / F Learning criminal behavior patterns is very different from learning conventional behavior patterns.

13. T / F Attachment involves the time, energy, and effort expended in conventional actions such as getting an education.

14. T / F Attachment refers to a person's sensitivity to and interest in others.

15. T / F In the testing of social control theory, youths who were strongly attached to their parents were less likely to commit criminal acts.

Fill in the Blank

1. Socialization is influenced by _____ and _____.

2. Children who have warm and affectionate ties to their parents report greater levels of _____ beginning in adolescence and extending into their adulthood.

3. Children who grow up in homes where parents use severe discipline yet lack warmth and involvement in their lives are prone to _____ behavior.

4. Schools contribute to criminality by _____ problem youths, which sets them apart from conventional society.

5. Religion binds people together and forces them to confront the _____ of their behavior.

6. Social learning theories assume that people are born _____ and learn to be _____.

7. _____ theory assumes that whether good or bad, people are controlled by the evaluations of others.

8. _____ theory assumes that people commit crime when their social learning leads them to perceive more definitions favoring crime than favoring conventional behavior.

9. People experience what Sutherland calls _____ when they are exposed to opposing attitudes toward right and wrong or moral and immoral.

10. Control theorist Walter Reckless argues that a strong _____ insulates a youth from the pressures of criminogenic influences in the environment.

11. The ties that bind people to society, including relationships with friends, family, neighbors, teachers, and employers is referred to as _____.

12. According to Hirschi, social control is measured by a person's _____, _____, _____, and _____.

13. Social reaction theory, also known as _____ theory, explains criminal careers in terms of destructive social interactions and stigma-producing encounters.

14. Negative labels _____ people and reduce their self-image.

15. Howard Becker refers to people who create rules as _____.

Essay

1. Explain the basic principles of differential association.

2. Discuss the testing and analysis of differential association theory.

3. Discuss the testing of neutralization theory

4. Discuss the validity of learning theories.

5. Discuss the supporting research and the opposing views on social control theory.

ANSWER KEY FOR CHAPTER REVIEW QUESTIONS

Multiple Choice

1.	(c) parental efficacy	p. 156
2.	(b) social process	p. 156
3.	(d) all of the above	p. 157
4.	(c) track	p. 157
5.	(a) social learning	p. 158
6.	(c) social control	p. 158
7.	(d) social reaction	p. 159
8.	(e) a and c only	p. 159
9.	(e) b and c only	p. 159
10.	(e) all of the above	p. 159
11.	(c) differential association	p. 160
12.	(e) all of the above	p. 160
13.	(b) the end justifies the means	p. 161
14.	(d) turn the other cheek	p. 161
15.	(b) drift	p. 162
16.	(a) denial of responsibility	p. 163
17.	(c) denial of victim	p. 163
18.	(d) condemnation of the condemners	p. 163
19.	(d) all of the above	p. 165
20.	(f) b and c only	p. 165

True/False

1.	False	p. 156
2.	True	p. 156
3.	False	p. 157
4.	True	p. 157
5.	False	p. 157
6.	True	p. 157
7.	True	p. 157
8.	True	p. 158
9.	False	p. 158
10.	False	p. 159
11.	True	p. 160
12.	False	p. 161
13.	False	p. 166
14.	True	p. 166
15.	True	p. 167

Fill in the Blank

1.	key social processes; institutions	p. 156
2.	self-esteem	p. 156
3.	antisocial	p. 157
4.	labeling	p. 157
5.	consequences	p. 158
6.	good; bad	p. 159
7.	social reaction	p. 159
8.	Differential association	p. 159
9.	culture conflict	p. 160
10.	self image	p. 165
11.	social bonds	p. 166
12.	attachment; commitment; involvement; belief	p. 168
13.	labeling	p. 168
14.	stigmatize	p. 169
15.	moral entrepreneurs	p. 169

Essay

1. pp. 159-61
2. pp. 161-2
3. pp. 163-4
4. pp. 164-5
5. pp. 167-8

8 Social Conflict Theory: It's a Class Thing

LEARNING OBJECTIVES

After mastering the content of this chapter, a student should be able to:

1. Understand the concept of social conflict and how it shapes behavior.
2. Discuss elements of conflict in the justice system.
3. Explain the idea of critical criminology.
4. Discuss the difference between structural and instrumental Marxism.
5. Discuss the various techniques of critical research.
6. Discuss the term left realism.
7. Understand the concept of patriarchy.
8. Explain what is meant by feminist criminology.
9. Discuss peacemaking.
10. Understand the concept of restorative justice.

KEY WORDS AND DEFINITIONS

Radical or Marxist criminology - The view that crime is a product of the capitalist system.

Conflict theory - The view that crime is a function of class conflict and power relations. Laws are created and enforced by those in power to protect their own interests.

Power - The ability of persons and groups to control the behavior of others, to shape public opinion, and to define deviance.

Instrumental Marxist - One who sees criminal law and the criminal justice system as capitalist instruments for controlling the lower class.

Demystify - To unmask the true purpose of law, justice, or other social institutions.

Structural Marxism - Based on the belief that criminal law and the criminal justice system area means of defending and preserving the capitalist system.

Surplus value - The difference between what workers produce and what they are paid, which goes to business owners as profits.

Marginalization - Displacement of workers, pushing them outside the economic and social mainstream.

Globalization - The process of creating a global economy through transnational markets and political and legal systems.

Left realism - Approach that sees crime as a function of relative deprivation under capitalism and favors pragmatic, community-based crime prevention and control.

Preemptive deterrence - Efforts to prevent crime through community organization and youth involvement.

Marxist feminism - Approach that explains both victimization and criminality among women in terms of gender inequality, patriarchy, and the exploitation of women under capitalism.

Patriarchal - Male-dominated.

Paternalistic families - Father is breadwinner and rule maker; mother has menial job or is homemaker only. Sons are granted greater freedom than daughters.

Role exit behaviors - Strategies such as running away or contemplating suicide used by young girls unhappy with their status in the family.

Egalitarian families - Husband and wife share similar positions of power at home and in the workplace. Sons and daughters have equal freedom.

Power–control theory - The view that gender differences in crime are a function of economic power (class position, one- versus two-earner families) and parental control (paternalistic versus egalitarian families).

Semiotics - The use of language elements as signs symbols beyond their literal meaning.

Deconstructionist - Approach that focuses on the use of language by those in power to define crime based on their own values and biases; also called postmodernist.

Postmodernist - Approach that focuses on the use of language by those in power to define crime based on their own values and biases; also called deconstructionist.

Peacemaking - Approach that considers punitive crime control strategies to be counterproductive and favors the use of humanistic conflict resolution to prevent and control crime.

Restorative justice - Using humanistic, non-punitive strategies to right wrongs and restore social harmony.

Sentencing circle - A peacemaking technique in which offenders, victims, and other community members are brought together in an effort to formulate a sanction that addresses the needs of all.

CHAPTER SUMMARY

Social conflict theorists view crime as a function of the conflict that exists in society. Conflict theorists suggest that crime in any society is caused by class conflict. Laws are created by those in power to protect their rights and interests. All criminal acts have political undertones. Richard Quinney has called this concept "the social reality of crime." One of conflict theory's most important premises is that the justice system is biased and designed to protect the wealthy.

Marxist criminology views the competitive nature of the capitalist system as a major cause of crime. The poor commit crimes because of their frustration, anger, and need. The wealthy engage in illegal acts because they are used to competition and because they must do so to keep their positions in society. Marxist scholars have attempted to show that the law is designed to protect the wealthy and powerful and to control the poor, have-not members of society. Among the branches of critical theory are instrumental Marxism and structural Marxism. The former holds that those in power wield their authority to control society and keep the lower classes in check. The latter maintains that the justice system is designed to maintain the status quo and is used to punish the wealthy if they bend the rules governing capitalism.

Research on critical theory focuses on how the system of justice was designed and how it operates to further class interests. Quite often, this research uses historical analysis to show how the capitalist classes have exerted control over the police, courts, and correctional agencies. Both critical and conflict criminology have been heavily criticized by consensus criminologists, who suggest that social conflict theories make fundamental errors in their concepts of ownership and class interest. New forms of social conflict theory have been emerging.

Feminist writers draw attention to the influence of patriarchal society on crime. According to power–control theory, gender differences in the crime rate can be explained by the structure of the family in a capitalist society. Left realism takes a centrist position on crime by showing its rational and destructive nature; the justice system is necessary to protect the lower classes until a socialist society can be developed, which will end crime. Postmodern theory looks at the symbolic meaning of law and culture. Peacemaking criminology brings a call for humanism to criminology. Conflict principles have been used to develop the restorative justice model. This holds that reconciliation rather than retribution should be used to prevent and control crime.

CHAPTER OUTLINE

I. The Conflict Theory of Crime
- A. Power Relations
- B. Research on Conflict Theory

II. Critical Criminology
- A. Origins of Critical Criminology
- B. Fundamentals of Critical Criminology
- C. Research on Critical Criminology
- D. Critique of Critical Criminology

III. Emerging Forms of Social Conflict Theory
- A. Left Realism
- B. Critical/Marxist Feminist Theory
- C. Power–Control Theory
- D. Postmodern Theory
- E. Peacemaking Criminology

IV. Social Conflict Theory and Public Policy
- A. The Concept of Restorative Justice
- B. The Process of Restoration
- C. Restoration Programs
- D. POLICY AND PRACTICE IN CRIMINOLOGY
  - 1. Practicing Restorative Justice
- E. The Challenge of Restorative Justice

CHAPTER REVIEW QUESTIONS

Multiple Choice

1. The view that crime is a product of the capitalist system is the basis of _____.
   a. radical criminology
   b. Marxist criminology
   c. biological criminology
   d. sociological criminology
   e. a and b only
   f. c and d only

2. Chambliss and Seidman documented how the justice system protects the _____.
   a. poor
   b. underclass
   c. rich
   d. powerful
   e. a and b only
   f. c and d only

3. Feminist scholars critically analyze _____.
   a. gender
   b. power
   c. criminality
   d. b and c only
   e. a, b, and c only

4. Critical criminologists view crime as a function of the _____ mode of production.
   a. capitalist
   b. communist
   c. socialist
   d. agrarian

5. Those in power use _____ as a tool to maintain their control over society.
   a. their wealth
   b. coercion
   c. the fear of crime
   d. none of the above

6. The poor are controlled through _____.
   a. unemployment
   b. incarceration
   c. death
   d. hunger

7. Those who see criminal law and the criminal justice system as capitalist instruments for controlling the lower class are referred to as _____ Marxists.
   a. Instrumental
   b. Structural
   c. Marginalized
   d. all of the above
   e. none of the above

8. Those who believe that criminal law and the criminal justice system are means of defending and preserving the capitalists system are referred to as _____ Marxists.
   a. Instrumental
   b. Structural
   c. Marginalized
   d. all of the above
   e. none of the above

9. Instrumental Marxists consider it essential to _____ law and justice.
   a. create
   b. expose
   c. challenge
   d. demystify
   e. none of the above
   f. b, c, and d only

10. The difference between what workers produce and what they are paid, which goes to business owners as profits, is known as _____.
   a. marginalization
   b. globalization
   c. surplus value
   d. none of the above

11. Displacement of workers, pushing them outside the economic and social mainstream is known as _____.
   a. marginalization
   b. globalization
   c. surplus value
   d. none of the above

12. The process of creating a global economy through transnational markets and political and legal systems is known as _____.
   a. marginalization
   b. globalization
   c. surplus value
   d. none of the above

13. Critical theory research is all of the following except _____.
   a. humanistic
   b. situational
   c. rigid
   d. descriptive

14. Recent developments in the conflict approach include all of the following except _____.
   a. legal realism
   b. biopsychology
   c. feminist theory
   d. power-control theory

15. Preemptive deterrence is an effort to prevent crime through _____.
    a. community disorganization
    b. youth involvement
    c. community organization
    d. a and b only
    e. b and c only

16. According to Marxist feminism, the exploitation of women is done by _____.
    a. everyone
    b. fathers
    c. husbands
    d. only elderly men
    e. b and c only

17. A male-dominated social system is referred to as _____.
    a. patriarchal
    b. matriarchal
    c. monarchal
    d. a dictatorship

18. According to Messerschmidt, capitalist society is marked by _____.
    a. patriarchy
    b. matriarchy
    c. class conflict
    d. low crime rates
    e. all of the above
    f. a and c only

19. Power-control theory claims that crime and delinquency are a function of _____.
    a. class position
    b. power
    c. family functions
    d. control
    e. all of the above
    f. none of the above

20. _____ families are characterized by the father as breadwinner and rule-maker and the mother has a menial job or serves as the homemaker.
    a. Paternalistic
    b. Maternalistic
    c. Monarchist
    d. Anarchist

True/False

1. T / F The ability of persons and groups to control the behavior of others, to shape public opinion, and to define deviance is referred to as bullying.

2. T / F According to conflict theory, definitions of crime favor those who control the justice system

3. T / F Research on conflict theory reveals that both white and black offenders have been found to receive stricter sentences if their personal characteristics show them to be members of the "dangerous classes."

4. T / F Research on conflict theory reveals that courts do not dole out harsher punishments to members of powerless, disenfranchised groups.

5. T / F Racism and classism shape crime rates according to conflict theory.

6. T / F Marx identified the economic structures in society that control all human relations. Marx planted the seeds of critical criminology.

7. T / F According to critical criminology, crimes of the helpless such as burglary and robbery are expressions of rage over unjust conditions.

8. T / F According to critical criminology, modern global capitalism helps destroy the lives of workers in less developed countries.

9. T / F All societies have consistent ways of dealing with criminal behavior.

10. T / F Critical theory research is more quantitative than qualitative.

11. T / F Left realists feel that police are wrongly accused of much of the police brutality citizens complain about.

12. T / F Postmodernists think language controls thought and behavior.

13. T / F Postmodernists believe that value-laden language can promote inequities.

14. T / F According to restorative justice principles, victims and the schools are central to justice processes.

15. T / F According to restorative justice principles, the first priority of justice processes is to assist the police.

Fill in the Blank

1. According to conflict theory, laws are created and enforced by those in _____ to protect their own interests.

2. Social conflict theory describes how power relations create _____ in U.S. society.

3. The _____ calls for a humanist version of justice.

4. The conflict definition of crime states that crime is a _____ concept designed to protect the power and position of the upper classes at the expense of the poor.

5. Instrumental Marxists' goal for criminology is to show how capitalist law preserves _____ power.

6. In a patriarchal system, women's work is _____.

7. Because women work within the household and in the labor market, they produce far greater _____ for capitalists than men.

8. According to Messerschmidt, the struggle of men to dominate women in order to prove their manliness is called _____.

9. _____ are the strategies such as running away or contemplating suicide used by young girls unhappy with their status in the family.

10. Peacemakers view the efforts of the state to punish and control as crime-_____ rather than crime-_____.

11. Peacemakers advocate _____ and _____ rather than _____ and _____.

12. _____ uses humanistic, nonpunitive strategies to right wrongs and restore social harmony.

13. Restoration involves turning the justice system into a "_____" process.

14. _____ rather than retribution should be used to prevent and control crime.

15. All criminal acts have _____ undertones.

Essay

1. Briefly discuss the branches of social conflict theory as depicted on p. 182 of your textbook.

2. Discuss the threat of globalization to the world economy.

3. Discuss the research on critical criminology including the critiques.

4. Use Marxist feminist theory to explain the violent abuse of women by men.

5. Evaluate power-control theory.

ANSWER KEY FOR CHAPTER REVIEW QUESTIONS

Multiple Choice

1.	(e) a and b only	p. 181
2.	(e) a and b only	p. 183
3.	(e) a, b, and c	p. 185
4.	(a) capitalist	p. 186
5.	(c) the fear of crime	p. 186
6.	(b) incarceration	p. 186
7.	(a) Instrumental	p. 187
8.	(b) Structural	p. 187
9.	(f) b, c, and d only	p. 187
10.	(c) surplus value	p. 188
11.	(a) marginalization	p. 188
12.	(b) globalization	p. 188
13.	(c) rigid	p. 190
14.	(b) biopsychology	p. 193
15.	(e) b and c only	p. 192
16.	(e) b and c only	p. 193
17.	(a) patriarchal	p. 193
18.	(f) a and c only	p. 193
19.	(d) all of the above	p. 195
20.	(a) Paternalistic	p. 195

True/False

1.	False	p. 183
2.	True	p. 183
3.	True	p. 184
4.	False	p. 184
5.	True	p. 184
6.	True	p. 184
7.	True	p. 184
8.	True	p. 185
9.	False	p. 186
10.	False	p. 190
11.	False	p. 192
12.	True	p. 196
13.	True	p. 196
14.	False	p. 199
15.	False	p. 199

Fill in the Blank

1.	power	p. 182
2.	inequities	p. 184
3.	peacemaking movement	p. 185
4.	political	p. 186
5.	ruling-class	p. 187
6.	devalued	p. 193
7.	surplus value	p. 193
8.	doing gender	p. 194
9.	Role exit behavior	p. 195
10.	encouraging; discouraging	p. 196
11.	mediation; conflict resolution; punishment; prison	p. 197
12.	restorative justice	p. 198
13.	healing	p. 199
14.	Reconciliation	p. 203
15.	political	p. 203

Essay

1. pp. 182-202
2. p. 189
3. pp. 189-91
4. pp. 193-4
5. pp. 195-6

9 Developmental Theories: Things Change

LEARNING OBJECTIVES

After mastering the content of this chapter, a student should be able to:

1. Explain the concept of developmental theory.
2. Discuss what is meant by a latent trait.
3. Discuss Gottfredson and Hirschi's general theory of crime.
4. Describe the concepts of impulsivity and self control.
5. Identify the factors that influence the life course.
6. Recognize that there are different pathways to crime.
7. Discuss the social development model.
8. Describe what is meant by interactional theory.
9. Understand the "turning points in crime."
10. Discuss the influence of social capital on crime.

KEY WORDS AND DEFINITIONS

Developmental theory - The view that criminality is a dynamic process, influenced by social experiences as well as individual characteristics.

Latent trait theory - The view that criminal behavior is controlled by a "master trait," present at birth or soon after, that remains stable and unchanging throughout a person's lifetime.

Life course theory - Theory that focuses on changes in criminality over the life course; developmental theory.

Latent trait - A stable feature, characteristic, property, or condition, such as defective intelligence or impulsive personality, that makes some people crime prone over the life course.

General theory of crime (GTC) - A developmental theory that modifies social control theory by integrating concepts from biosocial, psychological, routine activities, and rational choice theories.

Adolescent-limited - Offender who follows the most common criminal trajectory, in which antisocial behavior peaks in adolescence and then diminishes.

Life course persister - One of the small groups of offenders whose criminal career continues well into adulthood.

Pseudomaturity - Characteristic of life course persisters, who tend to engage in early sexuality and drug use.

Problem behavior syndrome (PBS) - A cluster of antisocial behaviors that may include family dysfunction, substance abuse, smoking, precocious sexuality and early pregnancy, educational underachievement, suicide attempts, sensation seeking, and unemployment, as well as crime.

Authority conflict pathway- Pathway to criminal deviance that begins at an early age with stubborn behavior and leads to defiance and then to authority avoidance.

Covert pathway - Pathway to a criminal career that begins with minor underhanded behavior, leads to property damage, and eventually escalates to more serious forms of theft and fraud.

Overt pathway - Pathway to a criminal career that begins with minor aggression, leads to physical fighting, and eventually escalates to violent crime.

Social development model (SDM) - A developmental theory that attributes criminal behavior patterns to childhood socialization and pro- or antisocial attachments over the life course.

Prosocial bonds - Socialized attachment to conventional institutions, activities, and beliefs.

Interactional theory - A developmental theory that attributes criminal trajectories to mutual reinforcement between delinquents and significant others over the life course—family in early adolescence, school and friends in mid-adolescence, and social peers and one's own nuclear family in adulthood.

Turning points - Critical life events, such as career and marriage, that may enable adult offenders to desist from crime.

Social capital - Positive relations with individuals and institutions, as in a successful marriage or a successful career, that support conventional behavior and inhibit deviant behavior.

Human capital - What a person or organization actually possesses.

Antisocial potential (AP) - An individual's potential to commit antisocial acts.

CHAPTER SUMMARY

Latent trait theories hold that some underlying condition present at birth or soon after controls behavior. Suspect traits include low IQ, impulsivity, and personality structure. This underlying trait explains the continuity of offending because, once present; it remains with a person throughout his or her life.

The general theory of crime, developed by Gottfredson and Hirschi, integrates choice theory concepts. People with latent traits choose crime over non-crime; the opportunity for crime mediates their choice. Life course theories argue that events that take place over the life course influence criminal choices. The cause of crime constantly changes as people mature. At first, the nuclear family influences behavior; during adolescence, the peer group dominates; in adulthood, marriage and career are critical. There are a variety of pathways to crime: some kids are sneaky, others hostile, and still others defiant.

Crime may be part of a variety of social problems, including health, physical, and interpersonal troubles. The social development model finds that living in a disorganized area helps weaken social bonds and sets people off on a delinquent path. According to interactional theory, crime influences social relations, which in turn influences crime; the relationship is interactive. The sources of crime evolve over time.

Sampson and Laub's age-graded theory holds that the social sources of behavior change over the life course. People who develop social capital are best able to avoid antisocial entanglements. Important life events or turning points enable adult offenders to desist from crime. Among the most important are getting married and serving in the military. According to David Farrington's ICAP theory, people with antisocial potential (AP) stand a greater chance of engaging in criminal offenses and remaining in a life of crime.

CHAPTER OUTLINE

I.   Latent Trait Theories
     A.   General Theory of Crime
II. Life Course Theories
     A.   The Glueck Research
     B.   Life Course Concepts
III. Theories of Criminal Development
     A.   The Social Development Model
     B.   Interactional Theory
     C.   Age-Graded Theory
     D.   CURRENT ISSUES IN CRIME
          1.   Tracking Down the 500 Delinquent Boys in the New Millennium
     E.   Integrated Cognitive Antisocial Potential Theory
IV. Evaluating Developmental Theories

CHAPTER REVIEW QUESTIONS

Multiple Choice

1.   _____ theory is the view that criminality is a dynamic process, influenced by social experiences as well as individual characteristics.
     a.   Developmental
     b.   Latent trait
     c.   Life course
     d.   None of the above

2.   _____ theory is the view that criminal behavior is controlled by a "master trait."
     a.   Developmental
     b.   Latent trait
     c.   Life course
     d.   None of the above

3.   _____ theory is the view that focuses on changes in criminality over the life course.
     a.   Developmental
     b.   Latent trait
     c.   Life course
     d.   None of the above

4. According to developmental theory, marriage and military service are _____ factors that can explain the onset and continuation of criminality.
   a. personal
   b. social
   c. socialization
   d. cognitive
   e. situational

5. According to developmental theory, information processing and attention/perception are _____ factors that can explain the onset and continuation of criminality.
   a. personal
   b. social
   c. socialization
   d. cognitive
   e. situational

6. Which of the following is not one of the criticisms directed at GTC?
   a. tautological
   b. personality disorder
   c. cross-cultural differences
   d. poor methodology

7. The GTC claims that _____ personality is key.
   a. weak
   b. strong
   c. psychotic
   d. impulsive

8. An offender who follows the most common criminal trajectory, in which antisocial behavior peaks in adolescence and then diminishes, is referred to as _____.
   a. adolescent-limited
   b. life course persister
   c. career criminal
   d. none of the above

9. One of the small group of offenders whose criminal career continues well into adulthood.
   a. adolescent-limited
   b. life course persister
   c. career criminal
   d. none of the above

10. According to _____, crime is just one among a group of antisocial behaviors that cluster together.
    a. the general theory of crime
    b. control theory
    c. problem behavior syndrome
    d. none of the above

11. The characteristic of life course persisters, who tend to engage in early sexuality and drug use is referred to as _____.
    a. prematurity
    b. immaturity
    c. pseudomaturity
    d. aging out

12. PBS involves all of the following except _____.
    a. family dysfunction
    b. substance abuse
    c. educational overachievement
    d. sensation seeking
    e. unemployment

13. PBS problem behaviors can be divided into the following forms except _____.
    a. social
    b. biological
    c. environmental
    d. personal

14. The pioneering _____ tracked the onset and termination of criminal careers.
    a. Gorings
    b. Sutherlands
    c. Blaus
    d. Gluecks

15. _____ is the pathway to a criminal career that begins with minor underhanded behavior, leads to property damage, and eventually escalates to more serious forms of theft and fraud.
    a. Authority conflict
    b. Covert
    c. Overt
    d. Aging out

16. _____ is the pathway to a criminal career that begins with minor aggression, leads to physical fighting, and eventually escalates to violent crime.
    a. Authority conflict
    b. Covert
    c. Overt
    d. Aging out

17. _____ is the pathway to criminal deviance that begins at an early age with stubborn behavior and leads to defiance and then to authority avoidance.
    a. Authority conflict
    b. Covert
    c. Overt
    d. Aging out

18. Sampson and Laub identify critical life events, such as career and marriage that may enable adult offenders to desist from crime. These critical life events are known as _____.
    a. event points
    b. life points
    c. crime points
    d. turning points

19. Sampson and Laub reanalyzed the original _____ data and found that the stability of delinquent behavior can be affected by events that occur later in life, even after a chronic delinquent career has been established.
    a. Sutherland
    b. Lombroso
    c. Glueck
    d. Thornberry

20. An individual's potential to commit antisocial acts is referred to as _____.
    a. antisocial personality disorder
    b. behavior potential
    c. antisocial potential
    d. all of the above
    e. none of the above

True/False

1. T /F People who carry suspected latent traits are in danger of becoming career criminals.

2. T /F In GTC, the offender and the criminal act are related concepts.

3. T /F Empirical research on GTC finds that people who commit white-collar and workplace crime have the same-level of control and non-offenders.

4. T /F The weakness of the GTC is its scope and breadth.

5. T /F The life course view is that criminality can best be understood as one of many social problems faced by at-risk youth.

6. T /F Those people who exhibit PBS are no more prone to behavior difficulties than the general population.

7. T /F Racism is a social form of PBS problem behavior.

8. T /F There is only one pathway to crime.

9. T /F Life course persisters begin offending late and age out of crime.

10. T /F According to life course theory, the best predictor of future criminality is past criminality.

11. T /F According to SDM, as children mature within their environment, elements of socialization control their developmental process.

12. T /F Interactional theory holds that causal influences are unidirectional.

13. T /F Building social capital supports conventional behavior and inhibits deviant behavior.

14. T /F People with a history of criminal activity who have been convicted of serious offenses reduce the frequency of their offending if they live with spouses and maintain employment while living in the community.

15. T /F AP is only a long-term phenomenon.

Fill in the Blank

1. GTC modifies and redefines some of the principles articulated in Hirschi's _____ theory.

2. Gottfredson and Hirschi trace the root cause of poor self-control to inadequate_____.

3. Impulsive people have _____ self-control and a _____ bond to society.

4. The life course view is that criminality can best be understood as one of many social problems faced by _____ youth

5. Family dysfunction is a _____ form of PBS problem behaviors.

6. Early sexuality is a _____ form of PBS problem behaviors.

7. _____ exhibit early onset of crime that persists into adulthood.

8. The _____ model is a developmental theory that attributes criminal behavior patterns to childhood socialization and pro- or antisocial attachments over the life course.

9. _____ are the socialized attachment to conventional institutions, activities, and beliefs.

10. _____ theory holds that seriously delinquent youths form belief systems that are consistent with their deviant lifestyle.

11. According to Sampson and Laub, two critical turning points that enable adult offenders to desist from crime are _____ and _____.

12. People who maintain a successful marriage and become _____ are the most likely to mature out of crime.

13. Marriage stabilizes people and helps them build _____.

14. According to ICAP theory, people with _____ stand a greater chance of engaging in criminal offenses and remaining in a life of crime.

15. According to Sampson and Laub's age-graded theory, building social capital and strong social bonds _____ the likelihood of long-term deviance.

Essay

1. Discuss the relationship between self-control and crime.

2. Why do some people enter a "path to crime" later rather than sooner?

3. Are there different pathways to crime? Discuss the three distinct paths to a criminal career.

4. Explain the life course theory assumption that criminal propensity may be "contagious."

5. Briefly discuss Sampson and Laub's Age-Graded Theory

ANSWER KEY FOR CHAPTER REVIEW QUESTIONS

Multiple Choice

1.	(a) developmental	p. 208
2.	(b) latent trait	p. 208
3.	(c) life course	p. 208
4.	(c) socialization	p. 208
5.	(d) cognitive	p. 208
6.	(d) poor methodology	pp. 211-2
7.	(d) impulsive	p. 213
8.	(a) adolescent-limited	p. 215
9.	(b) life-course persister	p. 215
10.	(c) problem behavior syndrome	p. 215
11.	(c) pseudomaturity	p. 215
12.	(c) educational overachievement	p. 215
13.	(b) biological	p. 216
14.	(d) Gluecks	p. 217
15.	(b) Covert	p. 217
16.	(c) Overt	p. 217
17.	(a) Authority conflict	p. 217
18.	(d) turning points	p. 221
19.	(c) Glueck	p. 221
20.	(c) antisocial potential	p. 226

True/False

1.	True	p. 208
2.	False	p. 209
3.	False	p. 212
4.	False	p. 213
5.	True	p. 215
6.	False	p. 216
7.	False	p. 216
8.	False	p. 217
9.	False	p. 217
10.	True	p. 217
11.	True	p. 218
12.	False	p. 221
13.	True	p. 222
14.	True	p. 222
15.	False	p. 226

Fill in the Blank

1.	social control	p. 209
2.	child-rearing practices	p. 210
3.	low; weak	p. 213
4.	at-risk	p. 215
5.	social	p. 216
6.	personal	p. 216
7.	Life course persisters	p. 217
8.	social development	p. 218
9.	Prosocial bonds	p. 219
10.	Interactional theory	p. 219
11.	career; marriage	p. 221
12.	parents	p. 222
13.	social capital	p. 222
14.	antisocial potential	p. 228
15.	reduces	p. 228

Essay

1. p. 211
2. p. 215
3. p. 217
4. p. 217
5. p. 223

10 Violent Crime

LEARNING OBJECTIVES

After mastering the content of this chapter, a student should be able to:

1. Explain the various causes of violent crime.
2. Discuss the concept of the brutalization process.
3. Discuss the history of rape.
4. Understand the different types of rape.
5. Discuss the legal issues in rape prosecution.
6. Recognize that there are different types of murder.
7. Discuss the differences between serial killing, mass murder, and spree killing.
8. Understand the nature of assault in the home.
9. Understand the careers of armed robbers.
10. Discuss newly emerging forms of violence such as stalking, hate crimes, and workplace violence.
11. Understand the different types of terrorism and what is being done today to combat terrorist activities.

KEY WORDS AND DEFINITIONS

Expressive violence - Acts that vent rage, anger, or frustration.

Instrumental violence - Acts designed to improve the financial or social position of the criminal.

Eros - The life instinct, which drives people toward self-fulfillment and enjoyment.

Thanatos - The death instinct, which produces self destruction.

Psychopharmacological relationship - The direct consequence of ingesting mood-altering substances.

Economic compulsive behavior - Drug users who resort to violence to support their habit.

Systemic link - A link that occurs when drug dealers turn violent in their competition with rival gangs.

Subculture of violence - Violence has become legitimized by the custom and norms of that group.

Rape - The carnal knowledge of a female forcibly and against her will.

Date rape - A rape that involves people who are in some form of courting relationship.

Marital exemption - Traditionally, a legally married husband could not be charged with raping his wife.

Statutory rape - Sexual relations between an underage minor female and an adult male.

Virility mystique - The belief that males must separate their sexual feelings from needs for love, respect, and affection.

Narcissistic personality disorder - A pattern of traits and behaviors that indicate infatuation and fixation with one's self to the exclusion of all others and the egotistic and ruthless pursuit of one's gratification, dominance, and ambition.

Aggravated rape - Rape involving multiple offenders, weapons, and victim injuries.

Consent - The victim of rape must prove that she in no way encouraged, enticed, or misled the accused rapist.

Shield laws - Laws that protect women from being questioned about their sexual history unless it directly bears on the case.

Murder - The unlawful killing of a human being with malice aforethought.

First-degree murder - Killing a person after premeditation and deliberation.

Premeditation - Considering the criminal act beforehand, which suggests that it was motivated by more than a simple desire to engage in an act of violence.

Deliberation - Planning a criminal act after careful thought rather than carrying it out on impulse.

Felony murder - A killing accompanying a felony, such as robbery or rape.

Second-degree murder - A person's wanton disregard for the victim's life and his or her desire to inflict serious bodily harm on the victim, which results in the victim's death.

Manslaughter - Homicide without malice.

Voluntary or nonnegligent manslaughter - A killing committed in the heat of passion or during a sudden quarrel that provoked violence.

Involuntary or negligent manslaughter - A killing that occurs when a person's acts are negligent and without regard for the harm they may cause others.

Infanticide - A murder involving a very young child.

Eldercide - A murder involving a senior citizen.

Serial killer - A person who kills more than one victim over a period of time.

Mass murderer - A person who kills many victims in a single, violent outburst.

Spree killer - A killer of multiple victims whose murders occur over a relatively short span of time and follow no discernible pattern.

Battery - Offensive touching, such as slapping, hitting, or punching a victim.

Assault - Does not require actual touching but involves either attempted battery or intentionally frightening the victim by word or deed.

Road rage - Violent assault by a motorist who loses control while driving.

Child abuse - Any physical or emotional trauma to a child for which no reasonable explanation, such as an accident or ordinary disciplinary practices, can be found.

Neglect - Not providing a child with the care and shelter to which he or she is entitled.

Child sexual abuse - The exploitation of children through rape, incest, and molestation by parents or other adults.

Robbery - Taking or attempting to take anything of value from the care, custody, or control of a person or persons by force or threat of force or violence and/or by putting the victim in fear.

Acquaintance robbery - A robber whose victims are people he or she knows.

Hate or bias crimes - Violent acts directed toward a particular person or members of a group merely because the targets share a discernible racial, ethnic, religious, or gender characteristic.

Workplace violence - Violence such as assault, rape, or murder committed at the workplace.

Stalking - A course of conduct directed at a specific person that involves repeated physical or visual proximity, nonconsensual communication, or verbal, written, or implied threats sufficient to cause fear in a reasonable person.

Terrorism - Premeditated, politically motivated violence perpetrated against noncombatant targets by subnational groups or clandestine agents, usually intended to influence an audience.

International terrorism - Terrorism involving citizens or the territory of more than one country.

Terrorist group - Any group practicing, or that has significant subgroups that practice, international terrorism.

Death squads - The use of government troops to destroy political opposition parties.

USA Patriot Act (USAPA) - An act that gives sweeping new powers to domestic law enforcement and international intelligence agencies in an effort to fight terrorism, to expand the definition of terrorist activities, and to alter sanctions for violent terrorism.

CHAPTER SUMMARY

Violence has become an all too common aspect of modern life. Among the various explanations for violent crimes are the availability of firearms, human traits, a subculture of violence that stresses violent solutions to interpersonal problems, and family conflict.

Rape, the carnal knowledge of a female forcibly and against her will, has been known throughout history, but society's view of rape has evolved. At present, close to 100,000 rapes are reported to U.S. police each year; the actual number of rapes is probably much higher. However, like other violent crimes, the rape rate is in decline. There are numerous forms of rape including statutory, acquaintance, and date rape. Rape is an extremely difficult charge to prove in court. The victim's lack of consent must be proven; therefore, it almost seems that the victim is on trial. Consequently, changes are being made in rape law and procedure. Rape shield laws have been developed to protect victims from having their personal life placed on trial.

Murder is defined as killing a human being with malice aforethought. There are different degrees of murder, and punishments vary accordingly. Like rape, the murder rate and the number of annual murders is in decline. Murder can involve a single victim or be a serial killing, mass murder, or spree killing that involves multiple victims. One important characteristic of murder is that the victim and criminal often know each other. Murder often involves an interpersonal transaction in which a hostile action by the victim precipitates a murderous relationship.

Assault, another serious interpersonal violent crime, often occurs in the home, including child abuse and spouse abuse. There also appears to be a trend toward violence between dating couples. Robbery involves theft by force, usually in a public place. Robbery is considered a violent crime because it can and often does involve violence. Newly emerging forms of violent crime include hate crimes, stalking, and workplace violence.

Terrorism is a significant form of violence. Many terrorist groups exist at both the national and international levels. There are a variety of terrorist goals including political change, nationalism, causes, criminality, and environmental protection. Terrorists may be motivated by criminal gain, psychosis, grievance against the state, or ideology. The FBI and the Department of Homeland Security have been assigned the task of protecting the nation from terrorist attacks. The USA Patriot Act was passed to provide them with greater powers.

CHAPTER OUTLINE

I.   The Causes of Violence
  A.   Personal Traits
  B.   Ineffective Families
  C.   Evolutionary Factors/Human Instinct
  D.   Exposure to Violence
  E.   Substance Abuse
  F.   Firearm Availability
  G.   Cultural Values

II.   Forcible Rape
  A.   History of Rape
  B.   Incidence of Rape
  C.   Types of Rapists
  D.   Types of Rape
  E.   The Causes of Rape
  F.   Rape and the Law

III.   Murder and Homicide
  A.   Degrees of Murder
  B.   The Nature and Extent of Murder
  C.   Murderous Relations
  D.   School Relations
  E.   Serial and Mass Murder

IV.   Assault and Battery
  A.   Nature and Extent of Assault
  B.   Assault in the Home

V.   Robbery
  A.   The Armed Robber

CHAPTER REVIEW QUESTIONS

Multiple Choice

1.　Killing a person after premeditation and deliberation is _____.
   a.　first degree murder
   b.　felony murder
   c.　second-degree murder
   d.　manslaughter
   e.　voluntary manslaughter
   f.　involuntary manslaughter

2.　A killing committed in the heat of passion or during a sudden quarrel that provoked violence is _____.
   a.　first degree murder
   b.　felony murder
   c.　second-degree murder
   d.　manslaughter
   e.　voluntary manslaughter
   f.　involuntary manslaughter

3.　A killing accompanying a felony, such as robbery or rape is _____.
   a.　first degree murder
   b.　felony murder
   c.　second-degree murder
   d.　manslaughter
   e.　voluntary manslaughter
   f.　involuntary manslaughter

4. Homicide without malice is _____.
   a. first degree murder
   b. felony murder
   c. second-degree murder
   d. manslaughter
   e. voluntary manslaughter
   f. involuntary manslaughter

5. More than _____ of the homicides occur in cities with a population of 100,000 or more.
   a. one quarter
   b. half
   c. three quarters
   d. 90 percent

6. Murder victims tend to be primarily _____.
   a. females
   b. males
   c. both males and females
   d. under the age of 21

7. The UCR indicates that about _____ children under 4 years of age are murdered each year.
   a. 500
   b. 1000
   c. 5000
   d. 8500

8. A person who kills more than one victim over a period of time is known as a _____.
   a. serial killer
   b. mass murderer
   c. spree killer
   d. none of the above

9. A killer of multiple victims whose murders occur over a relatively short span of time and follow no discernable pattern is known as a _____.
   a. serial killer
   b. mass murderer
   c. spree killer
   d. none of the above

10. A person who kills many victims in a single, violent outburst is known as a _____.
    a. serial killer
    b. mass murderer
    c. spree killer
    d. none of the above

11. The types of mass murderers include all of the following except _____.
    a. revenge killers
    b. love killers
    c. thrill killers
    d. profit killers
    e. terrorist killers

12. The types of serial killers include all of the following except _____.
    a. thrill killers
    b. mission killers
    c. expedience killers
    d. revenge killers

13. Female serial killers possess education levels that are _____.
    a. above average
    b. average
    c. below average
    d. extremely minimal

14. Since 1992, the number of assaults has _____.
    a. increased
    b. stayed the same
    c. decreased
    d. increased substantially

15. The NCVS indicates that only about _____ of all serious assaults are reported to the police.
    a. one quarter
    b. one half
    c. two-thirds
    d. three-quarters

16. The robbery rate is down more than _____ percent since 1992.
    a. 11
    b. 22
    c. 33
    d. 44
    e. 55

17. _____ states have the highest robbery rates by far.
    a. Western
    b. Southern
    c. Northeastern
    d. Southwestern
    e. Midwestern

18. Robbers use _____ to steal.
    a. stealth
    b. cunning
    c. force
    d. drugs

19. Suspected causes of rape include _____.
    a. male socialization
    b. hypermasculinity
    c. biological determinism
    d. all of the above
    e. none of the above

20. According to research, most hate crimes can be classified as _____.
    a. thrill motivated
    b. defensive
    c. retaliation
    d. mission-oriented

True/False

1. T / F Almost half of homicides occur in cities with a population of more than 1 million.

2. T / F Murderers tend to be males.

3. T / F The older the child, the greater the risk for infanticide.

4. T / F Although highly publicized in the media, the average annual incidence of school shootings is very small.

5. T / F Kids who have been the victims of crime themselves are the ones most likely to bring guns to school.

6. T / F The Washington-area sniper is an example of a mass murderer.

7. T / F Male serial killers are more likely to be substance abusers than their female serial killer counterparts.

8. T / F Battery does not require actual touching for it to occur.

9. T / F Assault involves intentionally frightening the victim by word or deed.

10. T / F It is difficult to estimate the actual number of child abuse cases because many incidents are never reported to the police.

11. T / F Women who were abused as children are at no greater risk to be re-abused as adults than those women who did not experience abuse as children.

12. T / F At all ages, slightly more girls than boys hit parents.

13. T / F Though most crime rates are higher in the summer, robberies seem to peak during the winter months.

14. T / F Patterns of assault are very different from those of homicide.

15. T / F Hate crimes usually involve convenient, vulnerable targets who are incapable of fighting back.

Fill in the Blank

1. Planning a criminal act after careful thought rather than carrying it out on impulse is referred to as _____.

2. Considering the criminal act beforehand, which suggests that it was motivated by more than a simple desire to engage in an act of violence, is referred to as _____.

3. A murder involving a very young child is known as _____.

4. A murder involving a senior citizen is known as _____.

5. Serial killer males _____ their victims while serial killer females _____ their victims.

6. Violent assault by a motorist who loses control while driving is known as _____.

7. Not providing a child with the care and shelter to which he or she is entitled in referred to as _____.

8. Parents are sometimes the target of abuse from _____.

9. Excessive _____ use may turn otherwise docile husbands into wife abusers.

10. Forcible rape has been known throughout history and is often linked with _____ and _____.

11. _____ are violent acts directed toward a particular person or members of a group merely because the targets share a discernible racial, ethnic, religious, or gender characteristic.

12. _____ stereotypes in films and on television are a factor that can produce hate crimes.

13. Workplace violence is now considered the _____ leading cause of occupational injury or death.

14. Violence such as assault, rape, or murder committed at the workplace is known as _____.

15. _____ usually involves a type of political crime that emphasizes violence as a mechanism to promote change.

Essay

1. How do murderous relations develop between two people who may have had little prior conflict?

2. Discuss the causes of child abuse.

3. Discuss the factors in child-to-parent violence.

4. Discuss why acquaintance robbery may be attractive for a number of rational reasons.

5. Discuss the potential motivations for hate crimes.

ANSWER KEY FOR CHAPTER REVIEW QUESTIONS

Multiple Choice

1.	(a) first degree murder	p. 246
2.	(e) voluntary manslaughter	p. 246
3.	(b) felony murder	p. 246
4.	(d) manslaughter	p. 246
5.	(b) half	p. 247
6.	(b) males	p. 247
7.	(a) 500	p. 247
8.	(a) serial killer	p. 249
9.	(c) spree killer	p. 250
10.	(b) mass murderer	p. 250
11.	(c) thrill killers	p. 250
12.	(d) revenge killers	p. 250
13.	(c) below average	p. 250
14.	(c) decreased	p. 251
15.	(b) one half	p. 252
16.	(d) 44	p. 254
17.	(c) Northeastern	p. 254
18.	(c) force	p. 256
19.	(d) all of the above	p. 256
20.	(a) thrill motivated	p. 259

True/False

1.	False	p. 247
2.	True	p. 247
3.	False	p. 247
4.	True	p. 249
5.	True	p. 249
6.	False	p. 250
7.	False	p. 250
8.	False	p. 251
9.	True	p. 251
10.	True	p. 252
11.	False	p. 253
12.	False	p. 254
13.	True	p. 255
14.	False	p. 256
15.	True	p. 258

Fill in the Blank

Essay

11 Property Crimes

LEARNING OBJECTIVES

After mastering the content of this chapter, a student should be able to:

1. Understand the history of theft offenses.
2. Recognize the differences between professional and amateur thieves.
3. Explain the similarities and differences between the different types of larceny.
4. Understand the different forms of shoplifting.
5. Discuss the concept of fraud.
6. Explain what is meant by a confidence game.
7. Understand what it means to burgle a home.
8. Discuss what it takes to be a good burglar.
9. Understand the concept of arson.
10. Discuss why people commit arson for profit.

KEY WORDS AND DEFINITIONS

Occasional criminals - Offenders who do not define themselves by a criminal role or view themselves as committed career criminals.

Situational inducement - Short-term influence on a person's behavior, such as financial problems or peer pressure, that increases risk-taking.

Professional criminals - Offenders who make a significant portion of their income from crime.

Larceny - Taking for one's own use the property of another, by means other than force or threats on the victim or forcibly breaking into a person's home or workplace; theft.

Constructive possession - A legal fiction that applies to situations in which persons voluntarily give up physical custody of their property but still retain legal ownership.

Petit (petty) larceny - Theft of a small amount of money or property, punished as a misdemeanor.

Grand larceny - Theft of money or property of substantial value, punished as a felony.

Shoplifting - The taking of goods from retail stores.

Booster - Professional shoplifter who steals with the intention of reselling stolen merchandise.

Fence - A receiver of stolen goods.

Snitch - Amateur shoplifter who does not self identify as a thief but who systematically steals merchandise for personal use.

Merchant privilege laws - Legislation that protects retailers and their employees from lawsuits if they arrest and detain a suspected shoplifter on reasonable grounds.

Target removal strategy - Displaying dummy or disabled goods as a means of preventing shoplifting.

Target hardening strategy - Locking goods into place or using electronic tags and sensing devices as means of preventing shoplifting.

Naive check forgers - Amateurs who cash bad checks because of some financial crisis but have little identification with a criminal subculture.

Systematic forgers - Professionals who make a living by passing bad checks.

False pretenses or fraud - Misrepresenting a fact in a way that causes a deceived victim to give money or property to the offender.

Confidence game - A swindle, usually involving a get-rich quick scheme, often with illegal overtones, so that the victim will be afraid or embarrassed to call the police.

Embezzlement - Taking and keeping the property of others, such as clients or employers, with which one has been entrusted.

Burglary - Entering a home by force, threat, or deception with intent to commit a crime.

Arson - The willful, malicious burning of a home, building, or vehicle.

CHAPTER SUMMARY

Economic crimes are designed to financially reward the offender. Opportunistic amateurs commit the majority of economic crimes. Economic crime has also attracted professional criminals. Professionals earn most of their income from crime, view themselves as criminals, and possess skills that aid them in their law-breaking behavior. A good example of the professional criminal is the fence who buys and sells stolen merchandise.

Common theft offenses include larceny, fraud, and embezzlement. These are common-law crimes, originally defined by English judges. Larceny involves taking the legal possessions of another. Petty larceny is typically theft of amounts under $100; grand larceny usually refers to amounts over $100. Larceny is the most common theft crime and involves such activities as shoplifting, passing bad checks, stealing, or illegally using credit cards. Some shoplifters are amateurs who steal on the spur of the moment, but others are professionals who use sophisticated techniques to help them avoid detection.

The crime of false pretenses, or fraud, is similar to larceny in that it involves the theft of goods or money; it differs in that the criminal tricks victims into voluntarily giving up their possessions. Embezzlement involves people taking something that was temporarily entrusted to them, such as bank tellers taking money out of the cash drawer and keeping it for themselves. Auto theft usually involves amateur joyriders who "borrow" cars for short-term transportation and professional auto thieves who steal cars to sell the parts that are highly valuable.

Burglary, a more serious theft offense, was defined in common law as the "breaking and entering of a dwelling house of another in the nighttime with the intent to commit a felony within. This definition has also evolved over time. Today most states have modified their definitions of burglary to include theft from any structure at any time of day. Because burglary involves planning and risk, it attracts professional thieves. The most competent have technical competence and personal integrity, specialize in burglary, are financially successful, and avoid prison sentences. Professional burglars are able to size up the value of a particular crime and balance it off with the perceived risks. Many have undergone training in the company of older, more experienced burglars. They have learned the techniques to make them "good burglars." Arson is another serious property crime. Although most arsonists are teenage vandals, others are professional arsonists who specialize in burning commercial buildings for profit.

CHAPTER OUTLINE

I. History of Theft

II. Contemporary Thieves

III. Larceny/Theft

    A. Shoplifting

    B. Bad Checks

    C. Credit Card Theft

    D. Auto Theft

    E. False Pretenses/Fraud

    F. Confidence Games

    G. Embezzlement

IV. Burglary

    A. The Nature and Extent of Burglary

    B. Types of Burglaries

    C. Careers in Burglary

    D. RACE, CULTURE, GENDER AND CRIMINOLOGY

        1. The Female Burglar

V. Arson

CHAPTER REVIEW QUESTIONS

Multiple Choice

1. By the 18th century, _____ moved freely is sparsely populated areas and transported goods, such as spirits, gems, gold, and spices, without paying tax or duty.
   a. skilled thieves
   b. smugglers
   c. poachers
   d. shoplifters

2. _____ make a significant portion of their income from crime.
   a. Professional criminals
   b. Career criminals
   c. Occasional criminals
   d. Shoplifters

3. Occasional property crime occurs when there is _____ to commit crime.
   a. professional skill
   b. opportunity
   c. situational inducement
   d. a and b only
   e. b and c only

4. By the end of the 18th century, _____ separate groups of property criminals were active.
   a. 3
   b. 5
   c. 8
   d. 10

5. Self-report studies indicate that a significant number of _____ have engaged in theft.
   a. males
   b. females
   c. juveniles
   d. elderly people

6. Larceny includes _____ larceny.
   a. miniscule
   b. petit
   c. grand
   d. shoplifting
   e. a and c only
   f. b and c only

7. English judges created the concept of constructive possession to get around the element of _____.
   a. forgery
   b. trespassing
   c. theft
   d. trespass in the taking

8. Fewer than _____ percent of shoplifting incidents are detected by store employees.
   a. 2
   b. 5
   c. 10
   d. 20

9. Which type of larceny is charged as a misdemeanor?
   a. grand
   b. petit
   c. personal
   d. property

10. Of the millions of property and theft-related crimes that occur each year, most are committed by _____.
    a. situational criminals
    b. occasional criminals
    c. professional criminals
    d. all of the above

11. _____ involve locking goods into place or having them monitored by electronic systems.
    a. Merchant privilege laws
    b. Target removal strategies
    c. Target hardening strategies
    d. All of the above
    e. None of the above

12. A person has _____ days to make a check good before they can be found guilty of passing a bad check.
    a. 2
    b. 10
    c. 20
    d. 30

13. In her pioneering study on shoplifters, Cameron found that about _____ percent of all shoplifters were professionals.
    a. 5
    b. 10
    c. 20
    d. 50

14. A majority of check forgers are _____.
    a. amateurs
    b. people who feel they are not hurting anyone
    c. naive
    d. all of the above
    e. none of the above

15. Amateur pilfers are called _____ in thieves' argot.
    a. boosters
    b. snitches
    c. fences
    d. targets

16. _____ are otherwise respectable persons who do not conceive of themselves as thieves but systematically steal merchandise for their own use.
    a. Boosters
    b. Snitches
    c. Fences
    d. Targets

17. To encourage the arrest of shoplifters, a number of states have passed _____ laws that are designed to protect retailers and their employees from lawsuits stemming from improper or false arrests of suspected shoplifters.
    a. citizen arrest
    b. clerk privilege
    c. merchant privilege
    d. target arrest

18. Lemert found that the majority of check forgers are _____.
    a. amateurs
    b. systematic forgers
    c. embezzlers
    d. opportunistic criminals

19. A few professionals make a substantial living by passing bad checks. Lemert referred to these persons as _____.
    a. amateurs
    b. systematic forgers
    c. embezzlers
    d. opportunistic criminals

20. The crime of _____ involves misrepresenting a fact in a way that causes a victim to willingly give his or her property to the wrongdoer, who then keeps it.
    a. embezzlement
    b. fraud
    c. larceny
    d. forgery

True/False

1. T / F Criminologists suspect that most economic crimes are the work of amateur criminals.

2. T / F Passing bad checks without adequate funds is a form of robbery.

3. T / F The original common-law definition of larceny required a "trespass in the taking."

4. T / F The American colonists created the concept of constructive possession to get around the element of "trespass in the taking."

5. T / F Grand larceny is punished as a felony.

6. T / F Auto theft adds up to more than $8 billion each year.

7. T / F Boosters are professional shoplifters who steal with the intention of reselling stolen merchandise to fences.

8. T / F Criminologists view shoplifters as people who are not likely to reform if apprehended.

9. T / F Embezzlement is entering a home by force, threat, or deception with intent to commit a crime.

10. T / F Unskilled and uneducated, urban burglars choose crime because they have few conventional opportunities for success.

11. T / F The crime of embezzlement was first codified into law by the English Parliament during the eighteenth century.

12. T / F Most active burglars avoid occupied residences, considering them high-risk targets.

13. T / F Most active burglars work in groups.

14. T / F Some burglars repeatedly attack the same target, mainly because they are familiar with the layout and protective measures.

15. T / F Professional burglars have careers in which they learn the tricks of the trade from older, more experiences pros.

Fill in the Blank

1. Professional theft includes _____, _____, and _____.

2. _____ was one of the earliest common-law crimes created by English judges to define acts in which one person took for his or her own the property of another.

3. Stores small and large lose at least _____ percent of total sales to thieves.

4. The majority of shoplifters are _____.

5. People who buy stolen property are called _____.

6. Professionals who make a living by passing bad checks are referred to as _____.

7. _____ percent of all auto thefts are reported to police.

8. Misrepresenting a fact in a way that causes a deceived victim to give money or property to the offender is referred to as _____.

9. _____ are run by swindlers who aspire to separate a victim from his or her hard earned money.

10. _____ occurs when trusted persons or employees take someone else's property for their own use.

11. _____ is the breaking and entering of a structure in order to commit a felony, typically theft.

12. The willful, malicious burning of a home, building, or vehicle is referred to as _____.

13. In the 18th century, _____ typically lived in the country and supplemented their diet and income with game that belonged to a landlord.

14. _____ thieves are opportunistic amateurs who steal because of situational inducements,

15. A shoplifter is also known as a _____.

Essay

1. Of the millions of property and theft-related crimes that occur each year, most are committed by occasional criminals. Other thefts, however, are committed by skilled professional criminals. Discuss the differences between these two types of criminals.

2. Discuss the nature and extent of burglary as portrayed by both the UCR and NCVS.

3. Discuss the various reasons for arson fraud.

4. Discuss how auto theft is combated.

5. Discuss typical confidence games.

ANSWER KEY FOR CHAPTER REVIEW QUESTIONS

Multiple Choice

1.	(c) poachers	p. 270
2.	(a) Professional criminals	p. 271
3.	(d) a and b only	p. 271
4.	(a) 3	p. 270
5.	(c) juveniles	p. 273
6.	(e) a and c only	p. 273
7.	(d) trespass in the taking	p. 272
8.	(c) 10	p. 274
9.	(b) petit	p. 273
10.	(b) occasional criminals	p. 271
11.	(c) target hardening strategies	p. 274
12.	(b) 10	p. 274
13.	(b) 10	p. 273
14.	(d) all of the above	p. 275
15.	(b) snitches	p. 273
16.	(b) Snitches	p. 273
17.	(c) merchant privilege	p. 274
18.	(a) amateurs	p. 275
19.	(b) systematic forgers	p. 275
20.	(b) fraud	p. 277

True/False

1.	True	p. 271
2.	False	p. 279
3.	True	p. 272
4.	False	p. 272
5.	True	p. 273
6.	True	p. 279
7.	True	p. 273
8.	False	p. 274
9.	False	p. 279
10.	True	p. 280
11.	False	p. 279
12.	True	p. 281
13.	True	p. 281
14.	True	p. 282
15.	True	p. 282

Fill in the Blank

1. shoplifting, extortion, forgery p. 271
2. theft, larceny p. 272
3. 2 p. 273
4. snitches and pilferers p. 273
5. fences p. 273
6. systematic forgers p. 275
7. 75 p. 276
8. false pretences or fraud p. 277
9. confidence games p. 278
10. embezzlement p. 279
11. burglary p. 282
12. arson p. 283
13. poachers p. 270
14. Occasional p. 271
15. booster p. 272

Essay

1. p. 271
2. pp. 279-80
3. p. 285
4. p. 277
5. p. 278

12 Enterprise Crime: White-Collar Crime, Cyber Crime, and Organized Crime

LEARNING OBJECTIVES

After mastering the content of this chapter, a student should be able to:

1. Understand the concept of enterprise crime.
2. Explain the similarities and differences between white collar crime, cyber crime, and organized crime.
3. Recognize the extent of the white-collar crime problem.
4. Describe the various types of white-collar crime.
5. Discuss the different approaches to combating white-collar crime.
6. Recognize new types of cyber crime.
7. Describe the methods being used to control Internet and computer crime.
8. Explain how organized crime developed.
9. List the different types of illegal behavior engaged in by organized crime figures.
10. Identify the newly emerging organized crime groups.
11. Explain how the government is fighting organized crime.

KEY WORDS AND DEFINITIONS

Enterprise crimes - Crimes of illicit entrepreneurship.

White-collar crime - Illegal activities of people and institutions whose acknowledged purpose is profit through legitimate business transactions.

Cyber crime - People using the instruments of modern technology for criminal purposes.

Organized crime - Illegal activities of people and organizations whose acknowledged purpose is profit through illegitimate business enterprise.

Sting or swindle - A white-collar crime in which people use their institutional or business position to bilk others out of their money.

Churning - Repeated, excessive, and unnecessary buying and selling of a client's stock.

Front running - Brokers place personal orders ahead of a large customer's order to profit from the market effects of the trade.

Bucketing - Skimming customer trading profits by falsifying trade information.

Insider trading - Using one's position of trust to profit from inside business information.

Influence peddling - Using one's institutional position to grant favors and sell information to which one's co-conspirators are not entitled.

Pilferage - Systematic theft of company property.

Corporate or organizational crime - Powerful institutions or their representatives willfully violate the laws that restrain these institutions from doing social harm or require them to do social good.

Actual authority - When a corporation knowingly gives authority to an employee.

Apparent authority - If a third party, such as a customer, reasonably believes the agent has the authority to perform the act in question.

Sherman Antitrust Act - Subjects to criminal or civil sanctions any person "who shall make any contract or engage in any combination or conspiracy" in restraint of interstate commerce.

Division of markets - Firms divide a region into territories, and each firm agrees not to compete in the others' territories.

Tying arrangement - A corporation requires customers of one of its services to use other services it offers.

Group boycott - An organization or company boycotts retail stores that do not comply with its rules or desires.

Price-fixing - A conspiracy to set and control the price of a necessary commodity.

Alien conspiracy theory - The belief, adhered to by the federal government and many respected criminologists, that organized crime is a direct offshoot of a criminal society.

Mafia - A criminal society that first originated in Italy and Sicily and now controls racketeering in major U.S. cities.

La Cosa Nostra - A national syndicate of 25 or so Italian dominated crime families.

Racketeer Influenced and Corrupt Organization Act (RICO) - An act that created new categories of offenses in racketeering activity, which it defined as involvement in two or more acts prohibited by 24 existing federal and 8 state statutes.

Enterprise theory of investigation (ETI) - Model that focuses on criminal enterprise and investigation attacks on the structure of the criminal enterprise rather than on criminal acts viewed as isolated incidents.

CHAPTER SUMMARY

Enterprise crimes involve criminal acts that twist the legal rules of commercial enterprise for criminal purposes. Enterprise crimes can be divided into three independent yet overlapping categories: white-collar crime, cyber crimes, and organized crime (see Concept Summary 12.1). White-collar crime involves illegal activities of people and institutions whose acknowledged purpose is profit through legitimate business transactions. Cyber crime involves people using the instruments of modern technology for criminal purpose. Organized crime involves illegal activities of people and organizations whose acknowledged purpose is profit through illegitimate business enterprise.

White-collar crimes include stings and swindles involving the use of deception to bilk people out of their money and chiseling customers, businesses, or the government. Surprisingly, many professionals engage in chiseling offenses. Other white-collar criminals use their positions in business and the marketplace to commit economic crimes, including exploitation of position in a company or the government to secure illegal payments, embezzlement and employee pilferage and fraud, client fraud, and influence peddling and bribery. Further, corporate officers sometimes violate the law to improve the position and profitability of their businesses. Their crimes include price-fixing, false advertising, and environmental offenses. So far, little has been done to combat white-collar crimes. Most offenders do not view themselves as criminals and therefore do not seem to be deterred by criminal statutes. Although thousands of white-collar criminals are prosecuted each year, their numbers are insignificant compared with the magnitude of the problem. The government has used various law enforcement strategies to combat white-collar crime. Some involve deterrence, which uses punishment to frighten potential abusers. Others involve economic or compliance strategies, which create economic incentives to obey the law.

Cyber criminals use emerging forms of technology to commit criminal acts. In some instances, they involve the use of technology to commit common-law crimes such as fraud and theft. In other instances, the technology itself is the target, for example, illegal copying and sale of computer software. Law enforcement officials fear that the incidence of cyber crime will explode in the future.

Organized crime supplies alcohol, gambling, drugs, prostitutes, and pornography to the public. It is immune from prosecution because of public apathy and because of its own strong political connections. Organized criminals used to be white ethnics—Jews, Italians, and Irish—but today African Americans, Hispanics, and other groups have become involved in organized crime activities. The old-line "families" are now more likely to use their criminal wealth and power to buy into legitimate businesses. There is debate over the control of organized crime. Some experts believe a national crime cartel controls all activities. Others view organized crime as a group of disorganized, competing gangs dedicated to extortion or to providing illegal goods and services. Efforts to control organized crime have been stepped up. The federal government has used antiracketeering statutes to arrest syndicate leaders. But as long as huge profits can be made, illegal enterprises will continue to flourish.

CHAPTER OUTLINE

I. White-Collar Crime
   A. Stings and Swindles
   B. Chiseling
   C. Individual Exploitation of Institutional Position
   D. Influence Peddling and Bribery
   E. Embezzlement and Employee Fraud
   F. Client Fraud
   G. Corporate Crime
II. Causes of White-Collar Crime
   A. Greedy or Needy?
   B. Corporate Culture Theory
   C. The Self-Control View
III. White-Collar Law Enforcement Systems
   A. Controlling White-Collar Crime

CHAPTER REVIEW QUESTIONS

Multiple Choice

1. _____ involves illegal activities of people and institutions whose acknowledged purpose is profit through legitimate business transactions.
    a. Organized crime
    b. Blue-collar
    c. White-collar crime
    d. All of the above

2. Corporate crime involves various illegal business practices such as _____.
    a. price-fixing
    b. restraint of trade
    c. false advertising
    d. all of the above
    e. none of the above

3. The categories of enterprise crime include all of the following except _____.
    a. white-collar crime
    b. cyber crime
    c. organized crime
    d. street crime

4. Distinguished criminologist Edwin Sutherland first used the phrase white-collar crime to describe the criminal activities of the rich and powerful in the _____.
    a. 1930s
    b. 1960s
    c. 1980s
    d. 1990s

5. A type of white-collar crime known as corporate crime includes _____.
   a. antitrust violations
   b. price-fixing
   c. false advertising
   d. all of the above
   e. none of the above

6. _____ involves people using the instruments of modern technology for criminal purposes.
   a. White collar crime
   b. Cyber crime
   c. Organized crime
   d. None of the above

7. Deception by individuals who use their institutional or business position to bilk people out of their money is an example of which category of white-collar crime?
   a. professional chiseling
   b. stings and swindles
   c. securities fraud
   d. influence peddling and bribery

8. Pharmacists have been known to alter prescriptions or substitute low-cost generic drugs for more expensive name brands. This is an example of which category of white-collar crime?
   a. professional chiseling
   b. stings and swindles
   c. securities fraud
   d. influence peddling and bribery

9. Which category of white-collar crime involves regularly cheating an organization, its consumers, or both?
   a. professional chiseling
   b. stings and swindles
   c. securities fraud
   d. influence peddling and bribery

10. All of the following but one are examples of securities fraud:
    a. churning
    b. front running
    c. bucketing
    d. morphing

11. In the late 1930s, the distinguished criminologist _____ first used the phrase "white-collar crime" to describe the criminal activities of the rich and powerful.
    a. Cesare Lombroso
    b. Emile Durkheim
    c. Edwin Lemert
    d. Edwin Sutherland

12. Blue-collar employees have been involved in systematic theft of company property. This type of theft is commonly called _____.
   a. bucketing
   b. churning
   c. front running
   d. pilferage

13. Organized crime includes _____.
   a. extortion
   b. loan sharking
   c. gambling
   d. all of the above
   e. none of the above

14. The victims of white-collar crime include _____.
   a. the general public
   b. the organization employing the offender
   c. a competing organization
   d. all of the above
   e. none of the above

15. A white-collar crime in which people use their institutional or business position to bilk others out of their money is known as a _____.
   a. swindle
   b. bilk out
   c. con
   d. sting
   e. a and b only
   f. a and d only

16. Abusive and deceptive health care practices include all of the following techniques except _____.
   a. ping-ponging
   b. gang visits
   c. steering
   d. driving

17. The Enron case is an example of _____.
   a. health care fraud
   b. educational fraud
   c. management fraud
   d. Internet fraud

18. Computer crime uses several common techniques. Which of the following is not one of these techniques?
   a. the Trojan horse
   b. the salami slice
   c. the logic bomb
   d. the super whammy

19. When this type of computer crime technique is used, an employee sets up a dummy account in the company's computerized records. A small amount is subtracted from each customer's account and added to the thief's account.
    a. the Trojan horse
    b. the salami slice
    c. the logic bomb
    d. the super whammy

20. Most organized crime income comes from _____.
    a. prostitution
    b. loan-sharking
    c. narcotics distribution
    d. all of the above

True/False

1. T / F White-collar crime involves the illegal distribution of legal material.

2. T / F Losses from street crime are higher than for white-collar crime.

3. T / F All three forms of enterprise crime involve violence.

4. T / F White-collar crimes today represent a range of behaviors involving individuals acting alone and within the context of a business structure.

5. T / F Using one's position of trust to profit from inside business information is referred to as churning.

6. T / F The control of workers' safety has been the province of the Environmental Protection Agency.

7. T / F The health care practice of referring patients to other doctors in the same office is called ping-ponging.

8. T / F Tax fraud is an easy study for criminologists because most people accurately report their income.

9. T / F Tax cheating is a serious crime and a great majority of major tax cheats are prosecuted because the IRS is a strong agent of the federal government.

10. T / F Stings and swindles involve long-term efforts to cheat people out of their money.

11. T / F The corporate culture theory can be used to explain the collapse of Enron.

12. T / F Cyber crimes cost consumers billions of dollars each year.

13. T / F The primary goal of organized crime is economic gain.

14. T / F Federal and state governments actually did little to combat organized crime until fairly recently.

15. T / F The Mafia is a major force in organized crime.

Fill in the Blank

1. Crimes of illicit entrepreneurship are referred to as _____ crimes.

2. White-collar crime, cyber crime, and organized crime are linked together because they involve _____.

3. According to the alien conspiracy theory, organized crime is made up of a national syndicate that call themselves _____.

4. In 1970, in an effort to control organized crime, Congress passed the
_____.

5. An individual convicted under RICO is subject to _____ years in prison and a $25,000 fine.

6. The major enforcement arm against environmental crimes is the _____.

7. If a computer is used to reprogram another for illicit purposes, the _____ technique has been used.

8. A conspiracy to set and control the price of a necessary commodity is referred to as
_____.

9. Detection of white-collar crime is primarily in the hands of _____ federal departments and agencies.

10. _____ theory suggests that some businesses actually encourage employees to cheat or cut corners.

11. White-collar enforcement may encourage _____.

12. Organizations that violate the law are given _____ fines.

13. Cyber crimes use _____ to commit crime.

14. _____ are lost each year on Internet fraud schemes.

15. The model that focuses on criminal enterprise and investigation attacks on the structure of the criminal enterprise rather than on criminal acts viewed as isolated incidents is called _____.

Essay

1. One important aspect of client fraud is tax evasion. Discuss what your text tells us about this form of white-collar crime. What must the government show to prove tax fraud? Explain when tax fraud is a felony and when it is a misdemeanor.

2. Internet crimes are a new breed of white-collar crime. Discuss at least four of the common techniques used to commit Internet crime.

3. Discuss what your text tells us about efforts to control computer crime.

4. There are a number of formal theories of white-collar crime. For this essay, you are to discuss the corporate culture view. Do you agree with this view of white-collar crime? Why or why not?

5. Discuss the causes of white-collar crime.

ANSWER KEY FOR CHAPTER REVIEW QUESTIONS

Multiple Choice

1.	(c) White-collar crime	p. 289
2.	(d) all of the above	p. 299
3.	(d) street crime	p. 289
4.	(a) 1930s	p. 290
5.	(d) all of the above	p. 297
6.	(b) Cyber crime	p. 289
7.	(b) stings and swindles	p. 291
8.	(a) professional chiseling	p. 292
9.	(a) professional chiseling	p. 292
10.	(d) morphing	p. 292
11.	(d) Edwin Sutherland	p. 290
12.	(d) pilferage	p. 294
13.	(d) all of the above	p. 290
14.	(d) all of the above	p. 291
15.	(f) a and d only	p. 291
16.	(d) driving	p. 295
17.	(c) management fraud	p. 295
18.	(d) the super whammy	pp. 306-7
19.	(b) the salami slice	p. 306
20.	(d) all of the above	p. 309

True/False

1.	True	p. 290
2.	False	p. 290
3.	True	p. 290
4.	True	p. 291
5.	False	p. 292
6.	False	p. 299
7.	True	p. 295
8.	False	p. 296
9.	False	p. 297
10.	True	p. 299
11.	True	p. 300
12.	True	p. 303
13.	True	p. 309
14.	True	p. 311
15.	False	p. 309

Fill in the Blank

1.	enterprise	p. 289
2.	entrepreneurship	p. 290
3.	La Cosa Nostra	p. 310
4.	Organized Crime Control Act	p. 313.
5.	20	p. 313
6.	Environmental Protection Agency	p. 299
7.	Trojan horse	p. 306
8.	price-fixing	p. 298
9.	administrative	p. 301
10.	Corporate culture	p. 303
11.	self-regulation	p. 303
12.	civil	p. 303
13.	technology	p. 307
14.	Billions	p. 307
15.	Enterprise Theory of Investigation	p. 313

Essay

1. p. 295
2. p. 306
3. p. 307
4. pp. 300-1
5. p. 299

13 Public Order Crimes

LEARNING OBJECTIVES

After mastering the content of this chapter, a student should be able to:

1. Explain the association between law and morality.
2. Discuss what is meant by the terms moral crusade and moral entrepreneur.
3. Discuss the legal problems faced by gay people.
4. Understand the constitutional cases that define gay rights.
5. Discuss what is meant by "obscenity."
6. Know the various techniques being used to control pornography.
7. Be able to discuss the various types of prostitution.
8. Know what is meant by the term paraphilias.
9. Discuss the history of drug abuse.
10. Be able to discuss the cause of substance abuse.
11. Identify the various drug control strategies.

KEY WORDS AND DEFINITIONS

Public order crime - Behavior that is outlawed because it threatens the general well-being of society and challenges its accepted moral principles.

Victimless crime - Public order crime that violates the moral order but has no specific victim other than society as a whole.

Moral entrepreneur - A person who creates moral rules, which thus reflect the values of those in power rather than any objective, universal standards of right and wrong.

Gay bashing - Violent hate crimes directed toward people because of their sexual orientation.

Homosexuality - Erotic interest in members of one's own sex.

Sodomy - Deviant forms of sexual intercourse.

Homophobia - Extremely negative overreaction to homosexuals.

Paraphilia - Bizarre or abnormal sexual practices that may involve nonhuman objects, humiliation, or children.

Prostitution - The granting of non-marital sexual access for remuneration.

Pornography - Sexually explicit books, magazines, films, or tapes intended to provide sexual titillation and excitement for paying customers.

Obscenity - Material that violates community standards of morality or decency and has no redeeming social value.

Temperance movement - The drive to prohibit the sale of alcohol in the United States, culminating in ratification of the Eighteenth Amendment in 1919.

Prohibition - The period from 1919 until 1933, when the Eighteenth Amendment to the U.S. Constitution outlawed the sale of alcohol; also known as the "noble experiment."

Narcotic - A drug that produces sleep and relieves pain, such as heroin, morphine, and opium; a habit-forming drug.

CHAPTER SUMMARY

Public order crimes are acts considered illegal because they conflict with social policy, accepted moral rules, and public opinion. There is usually great debate over public order crimes. Some charge that they are not really crimes at all and that it is foolish to legislate morality. Others view such morally tinged acts as prostitution, gambling, and drug abuse as harmful and therefore subject to public control. Many public order crimes are sex-related.

Although homosexuality is not a crime, homosexual acts are subject to legal control. Gay people are still not allowed to marry and are barred from the military and other groups such as the Boy Scouts. In 2003 the Supreme Court ruled that sexual relations between gay people cannot be criminalized. Prostitution is another sex-related public order crime. Although prostitution has been practiced for thousands of years and is legal in some areas, most states outlaw commercial sex. There are a variety of prostitutes, including streetwalkers, B-girls, and call girls. A new type of prostitution is cyber prostitution, which is Internet based. Studies indicate that prostitutes come from poor, troubled families and have abusive parents. However, there is little evidence that prostitutes are emotionally disturbed, addicted to drugs, or sexually abnormal. Although prostitution is illegal, some cities have set up adult entertainment areas where commercial sex is tolerated by law enforcement agents.

Pornography involves the sale of sexually explicit material intended to sexually excite paying customers. The depiction of sex and nudity is not illegal, but it does violate the law when it is judged obscene. Obscenity is a legal term that today is defined as material offensive to community standards. Thus, each local jurisdiction must decide what pornographic material is obscene. A growing problem is the exploitation of children in obscene materials (kiddie porn), which has been has expanded through the Internet. The Supreme Court has ruled that local communities can pass statutes outlawing any sexually explicit material. There is no hard evidence that pornography is related to crime or aggression, but data suggest that sexual material with a violent theme is related to sexual violence by those who view it.

Substance abuse is another type of public order crime. Most states and the federal government outlaw a wide variety of drugs they consider harmful, including narcotics, amphetamines, barbiturates, cocaine, hallucinogens, and marijuana. One of the main reasons for the continued ban on drugs is their relationship to crime. Numerous studies have found that drug addicts commit enormous amounts of property and violent crime. Alcohol is another commonly abused substance. Although alcohol is legal to possess, it too has been linked to crime. Drunk driving and deaths caused by drunk drivers are growing national problems. Strategies to control substance abuse range from source control to treatment. So far, no single method seems effective. Although legalization is debated, the fact that so many people already take drugs and the association of drug abuse with crime make legalization unlikely in the near term.

CHAPTER OUTLINE

I. Law and Morality
   A. Criminal or Immoral?
   B. Moral Crusaders
II. Homosexuality
   A. Attitudes Toward Homosexuality
   B. Legal Liabilities
   C. Is the Tide Turning?
III. Paraphilias
IV. Prostitution
   A. Incidence of Prostitution
   B. International Sex Trade
   C. RACE, CULTURE, GENDER AND CRIMINOLOGY
      1. The Natasha Trade: International Trafficking
   D. in Prostitution
   E. Types of Prostitutes
   F. Becoming a Prostitute
   G. Controlling Prostitution
   H. Legalize Prostitution?
V. Pornography
   A. Is Pornography Harmful?
   B. Does Pornography Cause Violence?
   C. Pornography and the Law
   D. Can Pornography Be Controlled?
VI. Substance Abuse
   A. When Did Drug Use Begin?
   B. Alcohol and Its Prohibition
   C. The Extent of Substance Abuse
   D. The Causes of Substance Abuse
   E. Drugs and Crime
   F. Drugs and the Law
   G. Drug Control Strategies
   H. Legalization

CHAPTER REVIEW QUESTIONS

Multiple Choice

1. Behavior that is outlawed because it threatens the general well-being of society and challenges its accepted moral principles is called _____.
   a. public order crime
   b. victimless crime
   c. social norm crime
   d. a and c only
   e. a and b only

2. _____ is the erotic interest in members of one's own sex.
   a. Sodomy
   b. Homosexuality
   c. Homophobia
   d. Eroticism

3. A person who creates moral rules, which thus reflect the values of those in power rather than any objective, universal standards of right and wrong is referred to as a _____.
   a. moral rights activist
   b. moral standard bearer
   c. moral entrepreneur
   d. moral leader

4. Sodomy refers to _____.
   a. a city mentioned in the Bible
   b. homosexual intercourse
   c. deviant intercourse
   d. a sexual orientation

5. The extremely negative overreaction some people have to homosexuals is called _____.
   a. homophobia
   b. homohater
   c. homoreactionist
   d. homopsychotic

6. Deriving pleasure from receiving pain or inflicting pain is referred to as _____.
   a. frotteurism
   b. voyeurism
   c. sadomasochism
   d. pedophilia

7. Prostitution that legally occurs in Nevada outside large population centers occurs in _____.
   a. hotels
   b. casinos
   c. brothels
   d. convention centers

8. In the case of _____, the U.S. Supreme Court determined that people could not be criminally prosecuted because of their status (such as drug addict or homosexual).
   a. Romer v. Evans
   b. Bowers v. Hardwick
   c. Robinson v. California
   d. Smith v. Atlanta

9. In the case of _____, the U.S. Supreme Court said that gay people couldn't be stripped of legal protection and made "strangers to the law."
   a. Romer v. Evans
   b. Bowers v. Hardwick
   c. Robinson v. California
   d. Smith v. Atlanta

10. Lower-class girls who get into prostitution report conflict with _____.
    a. school authorities
    b. poor grades
    c. an overly regimented school experience
    d. all of the above
    e. none of the above

11. Immoral acts are considered crimes when they cause _____.
    a. moral outrage
    b. majority outrage
    c. social harm
    d. community harm

12. Bizarre or abnormal sexual practices that may involve nonhuman objects, humiliation, or children is referred to as _____.
    a. paranormal
    b. paraphilia
    c. parapsychological
    d. parasite

13. Attaining sexual pleasure through sexual activity with prepubescent children is referred to as _____.
    a. frotteurism
    b. pedophilia
    c. voyeurism
    d. sadomasochism

14. Prostitution is illegal in all states except _____.
    a. California
    b. New York
    c. Nevada
    d. Texas

15. _____ is the rubbing against or touching a nonconsenting person in a crowd, elevator, or other public area.
    a. Voyeurism
    b. Frotteurism
    c. Pedophilia
    d. Exhibitionism

16. _____ is deriving sexual pleasure from exposing the genitals in order to surprise or shock a stranger.
    a. Voyeurism
    b. Frotteurism
    c. Pedophilia
    d. Exhibitionism

17. The arrest rate for prostitution reveals that the gender ratio is _____ female to male.
    a. 1:1
    b. 1:2
    c. 2:1
    d. 3:1

18. The aristocrats of prostitution are called _____.
    a. streetwalkers
    b. B-girls
    c. Brothel prostitutes
    d. Call girls

19. The newest form of prostitution is called _____.
    a. bar girls
    b. escort services
    c. call girls
    d. cyber prostitution

20. Prostitution was enforced by the _____.
    a. Temperance Act
    b. Volstead Act
    c. Prohibition Act
    d. Liquor Act

True/False

1. T / F To convict a person under the Miller doctrine, the state or local jurisdiction must specifically define obscene conduct in its statute, and the pornographer must engage in that behavior.

2. T / F Material that violates community standards of morality or decency and has no redeeming social value is referred to as obscenity.

3. T / F Prostitution is an emotional transaction.

4. T / F The Supreme Court has ruled that no material can be considered obscene.

5. T / F There is great debate whether obscene materials are harmful and are related to violence.

6. T / F More males than females actually engage in prostitution.

7. T / F Five times as many females as males are arrested for prostitution.

8. T / F Substance abuse is an ancient practice dating back more than 4,000 years.

9. T / F The Supreme Court has ruled that material is obscene if it has prurient sexual content and is devoid of social value.

10. T / F The "plant of joy," opium, was used over 4000 years ago is Mesopotamia.

11. T / F Prohibition was enforced by the Temperance Act.

12. T / F Prohibition was the period from 1919 until 1933, when the Sixteenth Amendment outlawed the sale of alcohol.

13. T / F There are indications that the DARE program is not overwhelmingly successful.

14. T / F Prohibition was also know as the "noble experiment."

15. T / F The cause of substance abuse can be either an environmental or a personal matter.

Fill in the Blank

1. Moral entrepreneurs create a climate where those categorized as _____ are deified while the _____ are demonized.

2. The line between behaviors that are merely immoral and those that are criminal are often _____.

3. Moral entrepreneurs often go on moral _____.

4. Deriving sexual pleasure from exposing the genitals in order to surprise or shock a stranger is referred to as _____.

5. The earliest record of prostitution appears in ancient _____.

6. Julia Roberts's character in *Pretty Woman* represents a _____.

7. The slang term for a prostitute, stemming from a Union general by the same name, is _____.

8. Sexually explicit books, magazines, films, or tapes intended to provide sexual titillation and excitement for paying customers are considered _____.

9. It is feared that some girls are forced or tricked into prostitution against their _____.

10. By the turn of the century, an estimated 1 million U.S. citizens were _____ users.

11. The _____ movement was the drive to prohibit the sale of alcohol in the United States in the early 1900s.

12. Those who view drug abuse as having an environmental basis concentrate on _____ addiction.

13. Parental drug abuse begins to have a damaging effect on children as young as _____ years old.

14. _____ appears to be an important precipitating factor in domestic assault, armed robbery, and homicide cases.

15. From a 2002 survey, about _____ violent crimes occurred each year in which victims were certain that the offender had been drinking.

Essay

1. Discuss the Supreme Court decisions involving homosexuality in the U.S.

2. Discuss what the research tells us about pornography and violence.

3. Is there a single "cause" of drug abuse?

4. Discuss the major drug control strategies that have been developed.

5. Discuss the drug/crime relationship. p. 344

ANSWER KEY FOR CHAPTER REVIEW QUESTIONS

Multiple Choice

1.	(d) a and c only	p. 317
2.	(b) Homosexuality	p. 320
3.	(c) moral entrepreneur	p. 319
4.	(c) deviant intercourse	p. 320
5.	(a) homophobia	p. 320
6.	(c) sadomasochism	p. 322
7.	(c) brothels	p. 326
8.	(c) *Robinson v. California*	p. 321
9.	(a) *Romer v. Evans*	p. 321
10.	(d) all of the above	p. 327
11.	(c) social harm	p. 320
12.	(b) paraphilia	p. 322
13.	(b) pedophilia	p. 322
14.	(c) Nevada	p. 328
15.	(b) Frotteurism	p. 322
16.	(d) Exhibitionism	p. 322
17.	(c) 2:1	p. 324
18.	(d) Call girls	p. 326
19.	(d) cyber prostitution	p. 327
20.	(b) Volstead Act	p. 333

True/False

1.	True	p. 333
2.	True	p. 328
3.	False	p. 323
4.	False	p. 331
5.	True	p. 331
6.	False	p. 324
7.	False	p. 324
8.	True	p. 338
9.	True	p. 331
10.	True	p. 332
11.	False	p. 333
12.	False	p. 333
13.	True	p. 341
14.	True	p. 333
15.	True	p. 334

Fill in the Blank

1. good; bad   p. 319
2. blurred   p. 320
3. crusades   p. 320
4. exhibitionism   p. 322
5. Mesopotamia   p. 323
6. streetwalker   p. 324
7. hooker   p. 324
8. pornography   p. 328
9. will   p. 331
10. opiate   p. 332
11. temperance   p. 333
12. lower-class   p. 334
13. 2   p. 335
14. substance abuse   p. 336
15. 1 million   p. 337

Essay

1. pp. 321-2
2. pp. 329-30
3. p. 336
4. pp. 339-43
5. pp. 339-43

14 The Criminal Justice System

LEARNING OBJECTIVES

After mastering the content of this chapter, a student should be able to:

1. Discuss the history of the criminal justice system.
2. Identify the component agencies of criminal justice.
3. Explain the various stages in the process of justice.
4. Understand how criminal justice is shaped by the rule of law.
5. Explain the elements of the crime control model.
6. Discuss the problem of prisoner reentry.
7. Discuss what is meant by the justice model.
8. Discuss the elements of due process.
9. Argue the merits of the rehabilitation model.
10. Understand the concept of nonintervention.
11. Explain the elements of the restorative justice model.

KEY WORDS AND DEFINITIONS

Criminal justice system - The agencies of government—police, courts, and corrections—responsible for apprehending, adjudicating, sanctioning, and treating criminal offenders.

Discretion - The use of personal decision making by those carrying out police, judicial, and sanctioning functions within the criminal justice system.

Landmark decision - A ruling by the U.S. Supreme Court that serves as a precedent for similar legal issues; it often influences the everyday operating procedures of police agencies, trial courts, and corrections institutions.

Adversary system - U.S. method of criminal adjudication in which prosecution (the state) and defense (the accused) each try to bring forward evidence and arguments, with guilt or innocence ultimately decided by an impartial judge or jury.

Prosecutor - Public official who represents the government in criminal proceedings, presenting the case against the accused.

Defendant - In criminal proceedings, the person accused of violating the law.

Convictability - A case that has a good chance of a conviction.

Defense attorney - The person responsible for protecting the constitutional rights of the accused and presenting the best possible legal defense; represents a defendant from initial arrest through trial, sentencing, and any appeal.

Right to counsel - The right of a person accused of crime to have the assistance of a defense attorney in all criminal prosecutions.

Public defender - An attorney employed by the state whose job is to provide free legal counsel to indigent defendants.

Pro bono - The provision of free legal counsel to indigent defendants by private attorneys as a service to the profession and the community.

Probation - The conditional release of a convicted offender into the community under the supervision of a probation officer and subject to certain conditions.

Incarceration - Confinement in jail or prison.

Jail - Institution, usually run by the county, for short-term detention of those convicted of misdemeanors and those awaiting trial or other judicial proceedings.

Prison or penitentiary - State or federally operated facility for the incarceration of felony offenders sentenced by the criminal courts.

Parole - A conditional early release from prison, with the offender serving the remainder of the sentence in the community under the supervision of a parole officer.

Arrest - The taking into police custody of an individual suspected of a crime.

Probable cause - Evidence of a crime, and of a suspect's involvement in it, sufficient to warrant an arrest.

Booking - Fingerprinting, photographing, and recording personal information of a suspect in police custody.

Interrogation - The questioning of a suspect in police custody.

Indictment - A written accusation returned by a grand jury charging an individual with a specified crime, based on the prosecutor's presentation of probable cause.

Grand jury - A group of citizens chosen to hear testimony in secret and to issue formal criminal accusations (indictments).

Preliminary hearing - Alternative to a grand jury, in which an impartial lower-court judge decides whether there is probable cause sufficient for a trial.

Arraignment - The step in the criminal justice process when the accused is brought before the trial judge, formal charges are read, defendants are informed of their rights, a plea is entered, bail is considered, and a trial date is set.

Bail - A money bond intended to ensure that the accused will return for trial.

Recognizance - Pledge by the accused to return for trial, which may be accepted in lieu of bail.

Plea bargain - An agreement between prosecution and defense in which the accused pleads guilty in return for a reduction of charges, a more lenient sentence, or some other consideration.

Hung jury - A jury that is unable to agree on a decision, thus leaving the case unresolved and open for a possible retrial.

Disposition - Sentencing of a defendant who has been found guilty; usually involves a fine, probation, or incarceration.

Appeal - Taking a criminal case to a higher court on the grounds that the defendant was found guilty because of legal error or violation of constitutional rights; a successful appeal may result in a new trial.

Courtroom work group - Prosecution, defense, and judges working together to resolve criminal cases quickly and efficiently through plea bargaining.

Law of criminal procedure - Judicial precedents that define and guarantee the rights of criminal defendants and control the various components of the criminal justice system.

Bill of Rights - The first 10 amendments to the U.S. Constitution, including guarantees against unreasonable search and seizure, self-incrimination, and cruel punishment.

Crime control model - View that the overriding purpose of the justice system is to protect the public, deter criminal behavior, and incapacitate known criminals; favors speedy, efficient justice and punishment.

Miranda rights - Rights of criminal defendants, including the right against self-incrimination and right to counsel, spelled out in the case of Miranda v. Arizona.

Exclusionary rule - The rule that evidence against a defendant may not be presented in court if it was obtained in violation of the defendant's rights.

Justice model - View that emphasizes fairness and equal treatment in criminal procedures and sentencing.

Determinate sentencing - Principle that all offenders who commit the same crime should receive the same sentence.

Due process model - View that focuses on protecting the civil rights of those accused of crime.

Rehabilitation model - View that sees criminals as victims of social injustice, poverty, and racism and suggests that appropriate treatment can change them into productive, law-abiding citizens.

Noninterventionist model - The view that arresting and labeling offenders does more harm than good, that youthful offenders in particular should be diverted into informal treatment programs, and that minor offenses should be decriminalized.

Restorative justice model - View that emphasizes the promotion of a peaceful, just society through reconciliation and reintegration of the offender into society.

CHAPTER SUMMARY

Criminal justice refers to the formal processes and institutions that have been established to apprehend, try, punish, and treat law violators. The major components of the criminal justice system are the police, the courts, and correctional agencies. Police maintain public order, deter crime, and apprehend law violators. Police departments are now experimenting with community and problem-oriented policing. The courts determine the criminal liability of accused offenders brought before them and dispense sanctions to those found guilty of crime. Corrections agencies provide post-adjudicatory care to offenders who are sentenced by the courts to confinement or community supervision. Dissatisfaction with traditional forms of corrections has spurred the development of community-based facilities and work release and work furlough programs. Justice can also be conceived of as a process through which offenders flow.

The justice process begins with initial contact by a police agency and proceeds through investigation and custody, trial stages, and correctional system processing. At any stage of the process, the offender may be excused because evidence is lacking, the case is trivial, or a decision maker simply decides to discontinue interest in the case. Procedures, policies, and practices employed within the criminal justice system are scrutinized by the courts to make sure they do not violate the guidelines in the first 10 amendments to the U.S. Constitution. If a violation occurs, the defendant can appeal the case and seek to overturn the conviction.

Among the rights that must be honored are freedom from illegal searches and seizures and treatment with overall fairness and due process. Several different philosophies or perspectives dominate the justice process. The crime control model asserts that the goals of justice are protection of the public and incapacitation of known offenders. The justice model calls for fair, equal treatment for all offenders. The due process model emphasizes liberal principles, such as legal rights and procedural fairness for the offender. The rehabilitation model views the justice system as a wise and caring parent. The noninterventionist perspective calls for minimal interference in offenders' lives. The restorative justice model seeks non-punitive, humane solutions to the conflict inherent in crime and victimization.

CHAPTER OUTLINE

I.   What Is the Criminal Justice System?
    A.   Police and Law Enforcement
    B.   The Criminal Court System
    C.   Corrections
II. The Process of Justice
III. Criminal Justice and the Rule of Law
IV. Concepts of Justice
    A.   Crime Control Model
    B.   CURRENT ISSUES IN CRIME
        1.   The Problems of Reentry
    C.   Justice Model
    D.   Due Process Model
    E.   RACE, CULTURE, GENDER AND CRIMINOLOGY
        1.   Race and Sentencing
    F.   Rehabilitation Model
    G.   Nonintervention Model
    H.   Restorative Justice Model
    I.   Concepts of Justice Today

CHAPTER REVIEW QUESTIONS

Multiple Choice

1. Approximately _____ law enforcement agencies operate in the United States.
    a. 10,000
    b. 13,000
    c. 17,000
    d. 20,000

2. Common criminal justice agencies have existed for only _____ years or so.
    a. 300
    b. 250
    c. 200
    d. 150

3. The agencies of the criminal justice system include _____.
    a. police
    b. courts
    c. corrections
    d. all of the above

4. Law enforcement agencies have been charged with _____.
    a. peacekeeping
    b. deterring potential criminals
    c. apprehending law violators
    d. a and c only
    e. a, b, and c
    f. none of the above

5. In recent years, police departments have experimented with new forms of law enforcement, including _____.
    a. community control
    b. community policing
    c. problem-oriented policing
    d. b and c only

6. _____ are the most visible agents of the justice process.
    a. Police
    b. Federal agents
    c. Secret Service Agents
    d. U.S. Marshals

7. The _____ are considered by many to be the core element in the administration of criminal justice.
    a. judges
    b. police
    c. criminal courts
    d. prosecutors

8. Most states employ a/an _____ court system.
   a. unitiered
   b. bitiered
   c. multitiered
   d. independent

9. Lower courts _____.
   a. try felony cases
   b. try misdemeanors
   c. review the criminal procedures of trial courts to determine whether the offenders were treated fairly
   d. all of the above

10. The U.S. Supreme Court is the court of _____ for all cases tried in the various federal and state courts.
    a. record
    b. cert
    c. last resort
    d. none of the above

11. Which courts are the trial courts of the federal system?
    a. U.S. district courts
    b. Intermediate federal courts of appeals
    c. The U.S. Supreme Court
    d. All courts in the federal system are trial courts.

12. The U.S. Supreme Court is composed of _____ members.
    a. 5
    b. 7
    c. 9
    d. 11

13. Within the structure of the court system, the prosecutor and the defense attorney are opponents in what is known as the _____ system.
    a. oppositional
    b. conflictual
    c. prosecutorial
    d. adversary

14. The federal court system has long provided counsel to the indigent on the basis of the _____ Amendment of the U.S. Constitution.
    a. First
    b. Fourth
    c. Fifth
    d. Sixth

15. The prosecutor is a public official who is _____.
    a. elected
    b. appointed
    c. either a or b
    d. neither a or b

16. The most common correctional treatment is _____.
    a. incarceration
    b. probation
    c. incapacitation
    d. parole

17. The provision of free legal counsel to indigent defendants by private attorneys as a service to the profession and the community is called _____.
    a. legal aid
    b. pro bono
    c. legal welfare
    d. none of the above

18. In about half the states and in the federal system, the decision to bring a suspect to trial is made by a group of citizens brought together to form a/an _____.
    a. preliminary hearing
    b. federal jury
    c. indictment hearing
    d. grand jury

19. _____ usually involves a fine, a term of community supervision, a period of incarceration, or in some cases a combination of these penalties.
    a. Arraignment
    b. Disposition
    c. Adjudication
    d. Investigation

20. _____ is the largest component of the criminal justice system.
    a. Law enforcement
    b. Corrections
    c. The court system
    d. none of the above

True/False

1. T / F Prisons hold those convicted of misdemeanors and those awaiting trial or those involved in other proceedings, such as grand jury deliberation, arraignments, or preliminary hearings.

2. T / F The first 10 Amendments to the U.S. Constitution, ratified in 1791, are generally called the Bill of Rights.

3. T / F The crime control model is rooted in the social learning theory.

4. T / F According to the justice model, it is futile to rehabilitate criminals.

5. T / F Crime control advocates see themselves as protectors of civil rights.

6. T / F The due process model embraces the notion that given the proper care and treatment, criminals can be changed into productive, law-abiding citizens.

7. T / F The nonintervention model calls for limiting government intrusion into the lives of people, especially minors, who run afoul of the law.

8. T / F The concept of a criminal justice system is relatively old

9. T / F The criminal justice process can be best understood as a series of decision points.

10. T / F The justice system is bound by the rule of law.

11. T / F Most criminal cases are resolved through plea bargaining.

12. T / F The restorative justice model is inspired by Zen and paramiltarism.

13. T / F The U.S. Supreme Court is composed of 9 appointed judges.

14. T / F Noninterventionists advocate institutionalization of non-serious offenders, diversion from formal court processes into formal treatment programs, and criminalization of non-serious offenses.

15. T / F Advocates of the restorative justice model say that state efforts to punish and control reduce crime.

Fill in the Blank

1. The U.S. Supreme Court is the _____ federal appeals court.

2. The most common correctional treatment is _____.

3. Another name for the _____ hearing is a probable cause hearing.

4. The criminal justice system can be compared to a _____ shape.

5. The crime control philosophy emphasizes protecting society and compensating _____.

6. U.S. Supreme Court Justices are appointed for _____ terms.

7. A _____ decision is a ruling by the U.S. Supreme Court that serves as a precedent for similar legal issues.

8. _____ is the conditional early release from prison, with the offender serving the remainder of the sentence in the community under the supervision of a _____ officer.

9. _____ is evidence of a crime, and of a suspect's involvement in it, sufficient to warrant an arrest.

10. _____ is the questioning of a suspect in police custody.

11. A group of citizens chosen to hear testimony in secret and to issue formal criminal accusations (indictments) is called _____.

12. A money bond intended to ensure that the accused will return for trial is called _____.

13. When the prosecutor, defense attorney, and judge work together to resolve criminal cases quickly and efficiently through plea bargaining, the group is called _____.

14. The principle that all offenders who commit the same crime should receive the same sentence is called _____.

15. The _____ model focuses on protecting the civil rights of those accused of crime.

Essay

1. Discuss the key concerns and concepts of justice.

2. Briefly discuss each of the decision points involved in processing a felony offender.

3. Discuss the use of discretion by criminal justice professionals.

4. Compare the traditional law enforcement role with the contemporary law enforcement role.

5. Compare and contrast the rehabilitation model and the nonintervention model.

ANSWER KEY FOR CHAPTER REVIEW QUESTIONS

Multiple Choice

1.	(c) 17,000	p. 352
2.	(d) 150	p. 350
3.	(d) all of the above	p. 350
4.	(e) a, b, and c	p. 352
5.	(d) b and c only	p. 353
6.	(a) Police	p. 352
7.	(c) criminal courts	p. 354
8.	(c) multitiered	p. 354
9.	(b) try misdemeanors	p. 354
10.	(c) last resort	p. 355
11.	(a) U.S. district courts	p. 354
12.	(c) 9	p. 355
13.	(d) adversary	p. 355
14.	(d) Sixth	p. 358
15.	(d) neither a or b	p. 356
16.	(b) probation	p. 358
17.	(b) pro bono	p. 358
18.	(d) grand jury	p. 362
19.	(b) Disposition	p. 362
20.	(a) Law enforcement	p. 359

True/False

1.	False	p. 358
2.	True	p. 365
3.	False	p. 366
4.	True	p. 367
5.	False	p. 370
6.	False	p. 371
7.	True	p. 374
8.	False	p. 359
9.	True	p. 365
10.	True	p. 365
11.	True	p. 365
12.	False	p. 374
13.	True	p. 355
14.	False	pp. 373-4
15.	False	pp. 374-5

Fill in the Blank

1.	highest	p. 355
2.	probation	p. 358
3.	preliminary	p. 362
4.	funnel	p. 364
5.	victims	pp. 366-7
6.	lifetime terms	p. 355
7.	landmark	p. 355
8.	parole; parole	p. 359
9.	probable cause	p. 360.
10.	interrogation	p. 361
11.	grand jury	p. 362
12.	bail	p. 362
13.	courtroom work group	p. 365
14.	determinate sentencing	p. 367
15.	due process	p. 370

Essay

1. p. 375
2. pp. 360-3
3. p. 353
4. p. 352
5. pp. 371-4